Pet Owner's Guide to

PUPPY CARE AND TRAINING

John & Mary Holmes

HOWELL
BOOK HOUSE

New York

HOWELL BOOK HOUSE
A Prentice Hall Macmillan Company
15 Columbus Circle
New York, NY 10023

MACMILLAN is a registered trademark of Macmillan, Inc.

Library of Congress Cataloging-in-Publication data

pet owner's guide to puppy care and training / john and mary holmes

Library of Congress catalogue card number: 94–73812
ISBN 0–87605–994–9

Manufactured in Hong Kong

10 9 8 7 6 5 4 3 2 1

Contents

Chapter One: TAKING ON A PUPPY   **6**
Making the choice; The responsibilities; The benefits; The right start; The importance of inheritance.

Chapter Two: THE NEW PUPPY   **10**
Preparations; Buying Equipment (Feeding bowls; Brush and comb; Collar and lead; Identification; Toys; Beds and Bedding; Dog crates); Finding a vet; Collecting your puppy; Arriving home; The first night; House-training.

Chapter Three: FAMILY LIFE   **19**
Puppies and children; Playing games; Helping with training; Puppies and babies; Puppies and other pets; A new puppy and the family dog; Puppies and cars; House rules.

Chapter Four: CARING FOR YOUR PUPPY   **33**
Feeding (Dietary needs; Choosing a diet; Supplements; Water); Mealtimes; Problem feeders); Exercise; Grooming; Types of coat; Nails; Teeth; Bathing.

Chapter Five: HEALTH MATTERS   **45**
Weekly checks; Vaccination; Internal parasites (Roundworms); External parasites (Fleas; Ticks); Diarrhoea; Giving medication (Pills; Liquid medicine).

Chapter Six: UNDERSTANDING YOUR PUPPY   **51**
The dog's mind; Association of ideas; Correction and reward; Strength of associations; Relating to other dogs; Instinct and intelligence; The herding instinct; The retrieving instinct; The hunting instinct; The guarding instinct; The Terrier breeds; Understanding instincts.

Chapter Seven: TRAINING EXERCISES   **62**
The recall; Lead training; The sit; The down; Play training (Jumping; Shaking hands; Begging; Catching; Speak on command; Hide-and-seek; Retrieving).

Chapter Eight: GROWING UP   **73**
The need for discipline; Reaching adolescence; The in-season bitch; The case for neutering; Dominance; A balanced relationship; Coping with bad behaviour; Avoiding;Temptation; Dogs and the countryside; Praise and stimulation.

When you take on a new puppy it is the start of a new and exciting relationship which will, hopefully, develop into true companionship.

About the authors

Professional dog trainers John and Mary Holmes have spent a lifetime working with dogs, breeding them, caring for them, and training them. They have helped many handlers to solve problems with their dogs, as well as training their own dogs for a wide range of tasks – from film and television work to Obedience competitions and farm work. They have bred and shown pedigree dogs under their Formakin kennel name, and they were responsible for importing the Australian Cattle Dog to Britain. John is an international championship show judge, and his appointments include judging at Crufts. He is a well-known contributor to the canine press, and has written books on training the family dog and the working dog. Mary has served on the committee of the Australian Cattle Dog Society and has edited their Newsletter for eight years.

Acknowledgements

Photographs have come from a number of sources, and they have made a major contribution to the book. Thanks to Sally Anne Thompson for all the photographs on puppy care and training, to Steve Nash and Carol Ann Johnson for assorted pictures, and to the Metropolitan Police for the photo of a working German Shepherd Dog. Special thanks to the readers of *Dogs Today*, especially Linda Jury, who have allowed us to use photographs of their pet dogs, and to the magazine's editor, Beverley Cuddy, for her kind co-operation.

Chapter One

TAKING ON A PUPPY

MAKING THE CHOICE
Taking on a puppy is a major responsibility and commitment, and it is something that should never be rushed into. With luck, you are looking forward to a relationship that will last twelve to fourteen years, so your choice of dog should never be decided on a whim or on an impulse. There is little doubt that the majority of dog problems arise because so many people buy the wrong puppy or dog. It is like marrying the wrong person – you either have to make the best of a bad job, or make a break and start again. However, the difference with owning a dog is that you have taken on an animal that is totally dependent on you for all its needs. This relationship should never be abused. The responsible dog owner must appreciate that if you take on a dog – it is for life.

THE RESPONSIBILITIES
The first responsibility is to the dog, who in return for the love and devotion he so willingly gives, deserves to enjoy a reasonable quality of life. To some people this means feeding the dog well, going for a daily walk, which is often on a lead, and giving a lot of love. In many ways, this type of existence does not sound unreasonable, but there are hidden dangers. It is the so-called love, provided in abundance, which leads some owners into over-pampering and overfeeding their dogs, slowly but surely shortening a dog's life.

In order to enjoy life to the full, your puppy needs mental as well as physical exercise. He needs to live like a dog, not like a human – rolling in the grass, and, in permitted areas, allowed to gallop freely without the restriction of a lead. It is becoming increasingly difficult to find open space where a dog can run free, but it is important to be able to provide suitable exercise for a young, healthy dog.

Your second responsibility is to other members of the community. The responsible dog owner must appreciate that there are people who do not like dogs, and sadly, there are people who are frightened of them. You may be confident that your big, friendly, bouncy puppy means no harm when he goes rushing up to a stranger – but to the person who does not understand dogs, this could be seen as threatening behaviour. Increasingly, legislation is being introduced to protect the non-dog owning public, and more than ever before, dog owners must ensure that their dog is under control at all times.

You must also be prepared to 'clean up' after your dog. This may not be the most pleasant aspect of dog-ownership, but it is deeply anti-social to leave dog mess in public places – and you may well face a heavy fine if you are found to be negligent.

Your third responsibility is to yourself and to your family. A puppy who is forced to live in a household where one person likes him and another does not, will grow up into a very unhappy dog, probably living in an equally unhappy household.

THE BENEFITS
Those of us who have always kept dogs have always known that they are good for us. Recently, scientific studies have confirmed this view. It is now widely accepted in medical circles that dog owners live longer than non-dog owners, they are less likely to suffer heart attacks, and recovery from major illness is quicker. Stroking a dog can immediately lower the blood pressure; patients in hospitals, retirement homes and psychiatric hospitals all benefit from visits from specially selected therapy dogs.

THE RIGHT START
Despite all the stated benefits, the relationship between dog and owner can go sadly wrong. In fact, most problems that dog owners have to cope with could, and should, be avoided by the use of a little common sense, and by starting off with the right puppy. Perhaps the most important point to remember is that more can be learned about a puppy from his ancestry than from the puppy himself.

This is why a purebred puppy is less of a 'pig in a poke' than a mongrel. At least you have some idea of what the purebred puppy will grow up to look like, which is impossible with a mongrel. We have owned some very good mongrels who have become famous film stars, but they were all acquired as adults, when we could see what they were like. Do not believe all that has been said about mongrels being healthier and more intelligent than purebred dogs – that is a dangerous generality.

A cross-breed – the progeny of two recognised breeds – is not a mongrel. We have had some great successes with first crosses, and the highest percentage of passes for Guide Dogs in Britain has been the Golden Retriever crossed with the Labrador Retriever.

Although a pedigree puppy is likely to grow up resembling his parents, that does not mean that all the puppies in the litter will have the same characteristics – far from it. But it is this false assumption that is probably the commonest mistake made by would-be puppy buyers, and it leads to many square pegs which will not fit into round holes!

THE IMPORTANCE OF INHERITANCE
So which breed should you have? There are some four hundred breeds of dog worldwide, and breed books have been written about most of the better-known breeds, containing detailed descriptions. The weakness of many breed books is that they are often written by enthusiasts who see their breed through rose-coloured spectacles. Moreover, the author is liable to be labelled as a traitor by fellow breeders if there should be so much as a hint of any weakness in the breed. As a result, the good points of the breed are very often stressed – or even exaggerated – and any bad points are ignored.

A puppy inherits his characteristics from both parents, but some of these are more inheritable than others. According to Dr Malcolm Willis, the well-known geneticist, the most inheritable characteristic of all is fear. This is not surprising when we consider that the dog is descended from the wolf. The bold, fearless wolf would very soon be a dead wolf, while the shy, furtive wolf would live to pass its genes on to

This Yorkshire Terrier puppy does not need as much exercise as the Rottweiler puppy pictured below. Toy dogs are suitable for those living in apartments, but they still need regular exercise and will enjoy a walk in the park.

All puppies look appealing, but this Rottweiler will develop into a large dog requiring plenty of exercise, a lot of food, and firm handling.

It is important to see a puppy with its mother, and, if possible, with its father, so you can get some idea of how your puppy will develop mentally and physically.

future generations. A fearful or nervous dog is almost invariably an unhappy dog. It can also be, and often is, a dangerous one. Nervousness is the cause of the vast majority of people, including children, being bitten by their own dogs. There is a tendency for some kind-hearted people to pick the shy puppy from a litter because they feel sorry for him. Our advice is, don't!

For the first six weeks or so of his life, a puppy is entirely under the influence of his dam. Experiments have shown that nervous bitches produce nervous puppies, even when these have been fostered from another bitch. Never buy a puppy without seeing him with his mother, and if the mother is not the sort of dog you would like to own, do not buy the puppy. Take time to look at lots of litters. If you make the right choice you will have many years of fun, pleasure and companionship to look forward to. If you make the wrong choice, you will have years to regret it.

Chapter Two

THE NEW PUPPY

PREPARATIONS

Once you have decided to take on a puppy, you will need to make quite a few preparations before your puppy arrives home. If possible, decide on the puppy's name in advance. Everything will be strange to him, and if all the family are trying out different names on him, he will only become confused. If you cannot come up with the right name, just call him 'Puppy' until you do. Nearly all pups are used to coming to the sound of "Puppy, puppy" when the breeder has been calling the litter, and so your puppy should respond to this.

Check the safety of both house and garden to ensure there are no hazards for an inquisitive puppy. Trailing electrical wires are a magnet to pups, and they can cause fatal accidents. Flimsy coffee tables, standing lamps, ornaments on low tables all constitute accidents waiting to happen. Make sure that anything either harmful or valuable is kept out of the puppy's reach. The garden will need to be well-fenced and puppy-proofed. Puppies are great escapologists; they can squeeze through the smallest of gaps with the greatest of ease. Make sure there are no slug pellets lying around. These are very attractive to dogs, but they are poisonous and can have disastrous consequences if eaten.

BUYING EQUIPMENT

FEEDING BOWLS

Your puppy will need two feeding bowls, one for food and one for water. Bowls made of stainless steel are recommended. Although they are more expensive than other types, they are virtually indestructible, and they are easy to keep clean. This last point is important, as eating or drinking from dirty bowls can quickly cause stomach upsets.

BRUSH AND COMB

Few small puppies need very much grooming. However, you should get your puppy used to a grooming routine before it becomes a necessity – particularly if you have a long-coated breed. At this stage, all you will need is a good-quality brush and comb. The puppy's breeder is the best person to advise you on this.

COLLAR AND LEAD

It is a good idea to get your puppy used to wearing a collar right from the start. Once he is used to a collar, you can start lead training. A light buckled leather or soft nylon collar is best, and you will need a fairly long, light but strong lead.

IDENTIFICATION

In the UK it is illegal for a dog to be in a public place without a collar and tag with a name and address on it. Many breeders now have their puppies tattooed before they are sold. This is an excellent idea; it gives the dog a permanent identification even if he should lose his collar and tag. Another form of identification is the microchip, which is painlessly implanted under the loose skin between the dog's shoulders. The application of this technology will assume greater importance as it becomes more familiar. There are currently moves by some national Kennel Clubs to make micro-chipping universally compulsory. However, there is some opposition to this, particularly as the price of micro-chipping is much higher than the cost of a tattoo.

TOYS

A puppy must chew – it is part of growing up. Pet shops are full of all sorts of canine toys and it is worth getting a few. Make sure they are good quality, as all too many pups have to undergo surgery to remove bits of rubber, etc. from their stomach after chewing unsuitable toys. The best sort to buy are those made of hard rubber; certain nylon chews are also good and safe. If you are buying a ball, make sure it is large enough so that it cannot be swallowed.

You can buy knotted ropes in a variety of sizes, which most pups love to chew and pull on, or you can buy some thick, cotton rope and make your own. Cheaper still are the cardboard centres of toilet and paper towel rolls, which are always popular with puppies!

BEDS AND BEDDING

A warm draught-proof bed is essential. There are numerous types of dog beds on the market, but until the pup has stopped growing – and chewing – a plain cardboard box is perfectly adequate. Place the box on its side so that it makes a safe 'den' for the puppy. Bedding needs to be warm and washable. We always use synthetic fleece fabric. This reflects body heat, it is non-allergenic and is difficult to chew. It is also free-draining, which means that you can put newspaper under it and the upper side stays dry.

Recently there has been concern that some synthetic fleeces cause static electricity which can be harmful to the dog. When you are buying a fleece, test for static by rubbing your hand over it. If you do not get any 'sparks', then it should be safe.

DOG CRATES

Last but not least, buy a folding dog crate. These are expensive but they last a lifetime, and the benefit both you and your dog will get from it should far outweigh the initial expense. Dog crates are very popular in the USA, but there is some resistance to them in the UK, with people throwing up their hands in horror and saying: "I certainly don't want to shut *my* puppy in a cage!" But that is not the purpose of a crate.

By nature, dogs like to have a 'den' which they can call their own. A crate makes a very satisfactory substitute. It is a great help with house-training, and it makes a safe refuge for the puppy when he wants to sleep, eat his dinner, escape from tiny, clutching fingers, rowdy teenagers, or even from you, his owner, if you are busy or

ABOVE: The best type of feeding bowls to buy are those made of stainless steel. They are easy to clean, and they are virtually indestructible.

RIGHT: There is a huge range of collars and leads to choose from. A puppy needs to get used to wearing a light buckled leather or a soft nylon collar from an early age. A long, light lead with a trigger hook is most suitable for a pup.

RIGHT: Puppies need to chew – it is part of growing up – but that does not mean that you want your best shoes ruined!

BELOW: Make sure you provide safe, suitable toys which your puppy can chew during teething.

in a bad mood!

A dog who is used to a crate will learn to be relaxed when shut up in a confined space. So if your dog ever has to stay overnight at the vet, or goes to stay in boarding kennels, he will suffer far less stress if he is crate-trained. In some countries it is illegal to transport a dog loose in a car, but in any case he will be far safer if he is in a crate. If you take your pup with you on a trip, most motels are happy to accept dogs if they know a crate is being used, as there is no risk of dirty carpets or chewed duvets.

If you really do not like the idea of a crate, then at least have a 'play-pen' for the puppy, which can be similar to a child's play-pen. Whether you have a play-pen or a crate, put newspaper down on the floor and provide a cosy bed inside and a favourite toy.

Never use the crate for punishment. The whole idea is for the puppy to have a den of his own to enjoy. Do not shut him up for long periods during the day, but start with just a few minutes and gradually increase the time. If you are busy around the house or going out for a short while, put the puppy in the crate for safety, but remember that the crate is a place of temporary refuge – it is *not* your puppy's home.

FINDING A VET

If you do not already know of a good veterinarian in your area, you will need to find one before your puppy arrives home. If you have bought your puppy locally, the breeder will probably be able to help, or you can ask other dog-owning friends for a referral in your neighbourhood.

Go along and see the vet before you bring the puppy home. Some puppies may have received their first inoculation, but you will need to find out what the inoculation programme is in your neighbourhood. Your puppy will almost certainly have started a worming programme, but you will need advice about worming treatments over the next six months. A number of veterinary practices run 'Puppy Parties', which are great for socialising puppies, so you can ask about this at the same time.

In Britain, many breeders provide insurance to cover the first few weeks after the puppy goes to his new home. You may decide to continue this, and there are many companies that provide an insurance package. Your vet will probably have information on the deals available.

COLLECTING YOUR PUPPY

Try to collect your puppy early in the day so that he will have time to settle in before evening. Take a friend or a member of the family along with you to help. There are different opinions as to the best way to transport the pup. We would never put a puppy straight into a crate or a box in the back of the car. It seems cruel to take the pup away from his mother and siblings and then put him in a strange place and drive off. You want this puppy to like you and trust you – and this does not seem like a good start!

We suggest that you settle the puppy in your friend's lap, or if it is a big puppy, let him lie next to your companion on the seat. Put a collar and lead on your puppy. In the excitement of arriving home, the pup could easily slip out of the car, which is the last thing you need. Take along plenty of newspaper and old towels. Then, if the pup vomits – and he probably will – any mess can be mopped up without any trouble. Do not reprimand the puppy for being sick – it is not his fault.

Make sure you have all the necessary paperwork, such as vaccination certificates, record of worming, pedigree and transfer of ownership form (if applicable), and a certificate of tattooing or microchipping if this has been done. You will also need a diet sheet, and most breeders will willingly supply you with enough food for the first few days.

ARRIVING HOME

Take the pup out quietly and let him explore the garden. Do not ask all your neighbours and friends to come and admire him, and try to pick a time when the children are at school! Your puppy will have quite enough to get used to without being overwhelmed by lots of new people.

Once your puppy has relieved himself, he can be taken into the house, preferably confined to the kitchen or utility room. Offer the puppy a meal, play with him, and when he is relaxed and hopefully tired, let him sleep.

THE FIRST NIGHT

You should have already decided where the puppy is to sleep, and this will probably be the kitchen or utility room. If you are using a crate, make sure it is ready with a bed inside and the door open. Your puppy can have his first meal there, and you can encourage him to go in and have a nap during the day.

At night, take your puppy out to relieve himself just before you go to bed, and have a game with him in the hope of making him tired. Then, put the pup to bed with a toy. He is bound to miss his siblings and the familiar surroundings. We have found that a well-wrapped hot-water bottle (not too hot) and an old alarm clock, which will help to break the silence, can both be useful. The puppy will almost certainly whine or yap, but, if you are lucky, he will soon settle down.

However, some pups can keep on whining for hours and hours. Do not go and smack your puppy; he is not doing it to annoy you – the poor puppy is homesick. However, do not make the mistake of going to give him a cuddle. This will just make him shout louder in the hope that you will come back again. If you really cannot stand the noise, take the puppy, in his crate, into your bedroom. Once he is used to the crate during the daytime you can gradually get him used to staying in another room at night. Do not take the puppy on to or into your bed. You could be storing up trouble in the future, especially if your baby pup is going to grow into a sizeable adult!

HOUSE-TRAINING

All young animals born in nests *want* to keep their living quarters clean. This is why it is easy to house-train a pig, but almost impossible to house-train a chimpanzee! No one wants a dog to be dirty in the house but, approached sensibly, house-training should be no big problem. Do not start nagging at the puppy the minute you get him home, and do not make a drama out of it. Puppies who have been properly reared, with the opportunity to go outside to relieve themselves, or those used to going on paper, are usually easy to teach.

First, decide on the area of the garden or yard you want your puppy to use. Then choose a word or phrase to use to encourage him to do what you want. We use

A dog crate is an invaluable item of equipment. It gives the puppy a safe haven, and it is a useful aid when it comes to house-training.

When you collect your puppy, try to enlist the help of a friend to look after the newcomer on the journey home.

Allow your puppy to explore the garden when he first arrives home.

You can offer a meal, but do not worry if your puppy does not appear to be hungry. He should soon make up for lost time when he feels more settled!

"Hurry up"; some people use "Get busy". It does not matter what you say, so long as you always use the same words. Never put the puppy out alone. Always go with him, and stay with him, until he performs. Tell him to "Hurry up" in an encouraging tone, and as soon as he does what you want, repeat the phrase and give him lots of praise.

Do not be in too much of a hurry to rush back inside. Many pups, and adult dogs, eliminate more than once, so give your puppy a chance to empty his bowels completely. Then have a short game, and go back inside. You should soon be able to judge how long you need to stay out with the pup. Puppies usually give signs of wanting to relieve themselves. Some turn around and around, others sniff the ground, scratch, look around, whine, or suddenly squat down. An observant owner – and you will need to be one – soon learns what to look out for.

Puppies are fed a lot of food at frequent intervals, which means they need to urinate and defecate far more often than an adult dog. Additionally, puppies do not have much control over their 'insides' while they are still young, which means you have to be very quick to catch them before they have an accident on your best carpet. Your pup will need to go out after every meal, after a drink, as soon as he wakes up, after a game, and any other times he shows signs of uneasiness.

To start with, your puppy will be unable to last all through the night. Some conscientious owners get up during the night and take the puppy out, which undoubtedly speeds up house-training. But do not worry if you are not the sort who relishes waking up at 2am. Leave some newspaper on the floor, and if your puppy dirties the paper during the night, just clean it up; he should eventually grow out of it. To avoid mistakes during the day, shut the pup in his crate if you are too busy to keep an eye on him. As already stated, do not leave him for too long, and if you hear him scratching or whining, hurry back and take him out. If your puppy makes a mistake in the house when you are not there, do not punish him as he will have no idea what he has done wrong.

Occasionally, a puppy may not seem to have inherited the instinct to be clean, or the instinct has been weakened because the puppy has been forced to live under conditions where he had no alternative to being dirty. With this pup you will need to be even more vigilant. As soon as you see any signs of him squatting, pick him up very quickly, telling him "No" in a harsh voice, and take him outside. Do not shout – it will not help. Stay with the puppy, even if it is a long wait. Tell him to "Hurry up", and when he finally performs, make a really great fuss of him, telling him how clever he is.

Most pups soon respond to this, but if you have a really difficult pup, you will have to be a bit more severe. When you pick the puppy up, give him a shake and an even harsher "No". Even the most awkward pup will get the message sooner or later. However, remain vigilant at all times, and never forget to praise your puppy when he does the right thing.

Chapter Three

FAMILY LIFE

PUPPIES AND CHILDREN

Children and puppies should have a natural affinity with each other, and children should have the chance to interact with dogs from an early age. It has been proved that children who play with animals early in life tend to be more open-minded and make more effort to understand others, than children who have not had this opportunity. Puppies and children growing up together can form a lasting and rewarding relationship.

However, you must use common sense. No matter how accustomed to dogs your children are, nor how good-tempered your puppy, never leave a small child or baby alone with a puppy. Disasters can – and do – happen very quickly. A large pup can push a toddler over, and that child may be frightened of dogs for life. Sharp puppy teeth can easily puncture a baby's skin, unintentionally, but still painfully. Small hands clutching a tiny puppy can really hurt; and a child who does not know how to pick up a puppy properly may drop it.

If you do not have any children of your own, then beg, borrow or steal some! With all the anti-dog laws, now common in most places, it is vital that your puppy learns to associate with children. If there is a puppy class near you, then join as soon as you can so that you have the chance of socialising your puppy with other pups and children under controlled conditions. If you have friends with children, ask them to visit and play with the pup. If your pup is reluctant to go to children, do not force him. Take time, use plenty of praise and treats, and make sure your puppy only meets children who are good with dogs until he is comfortable with them.

If you have children of your own they must be taught to respect the pup and not treat him as a toy to be picked up, carried about and then dropped on the floor. Make sure the children learn to leave the pup alone when he is in his crate or sleeping in his bed, and when he is eating.

PLAYING GAMES

Most children and pups get a lot of fun out of playing together and it is good for both of them, but games with young children should always be supervised. Play involving rough-and-tumble should be avoided as the pup gets more and more excited, and the children usually end up in tears. If a child hurts another child in play, the 'victim' will usually retaliate by hitting back. The only way a dog can retaliate is with his teeth – and the consequences of this could be disastrous.

Once the pup knows his name, hide-and-seek is a good game for the children to play. One child can hold the pup while the other runs and hides behind a bush in the

Puppies are used to playing together in the litter, so they will enjoy games with their new human family.

This little girl is used to playing with a lively puppy, but supervision is essential so that the puppy does not become over-excited, which could frighten the child.

If you have a small pet such as a guinea pig, make sure the puppy does not alarm it by rushing up and yapping.

Dogs and cats brought up together can become the best of friends.

garden, or behind a door in the house. When the 'hider' calls the pup, the other child can let him go. Once the pup is doing this, he can have his eyes hidden while the child hides, and he can start 'searching' with his nose.

Tug-of-war games, especially with larger pups, are popular, but make sure the child always wins and take the tug toy away when the game is finished. Many pups enjoy retrieving, and a ball can supply endless pleasure to both pups and children. Chasing games may be fun, but they are not always a good idea. Pups love chasing and being chased, but unless the pup is called up during the game, rewarded and the game restarted, it is easy to end up with a pup who refuses to be caught.

HELPING WITH TRAINING

Children develop at different ages, but most over the age of seven or eight can help with training. When it is the pup's feed time, let the child call the pup and ask him to sit (See Chapter Six: Basic Training), and then reward him with his food. Children can also practice the 'Down' using a treat as a reward. But make sure this is not done too often; once or twice is enough.

Older children should be able to take the puppy out on a lead, although they should be accompanied by an adult. Young children tend to drag small pups along at excessive speed, or be dragged along by large pups, so an adult needs to supervise.

PUPPIES AND BABIES

It may well happen that before the pup is adult, a new baby arrives in the family. To a puppy or a dog, a baby is a very different creature from an older child. The parents are unlikely to regard their new pride and joy as an animal – but the puppy certainly will do just that! In this situation you may come across one of the few canine instincts which is really human – jealousy.

If you consider how many children become jealous of a new baby you should be able to sympathise with the puppy, but unfortunately many parents do not. If the pup shows any sign of resentment then he is accused of 'turning nasty'; he is therefore treated harshly, which simply makes matters worse. This is not really the parents' fault, as they will instinctively feel protective towards the new arrival.

In most cases it is not the love and affection lavished on the baby that cause the trouble, but the change in attitude towards the puppy. Do not assume that every pup will be jealous of a new baby; a great many are not – but you should be prepared. The best course of action is to introduce your puppy to some friends' babies before the arrival of yours. However, if that is not possible, try to make sure that the puppy is not left out of things; let him see that the baby is now part of the family, just as he is. Do not shut the puppy away when the baby is being fed, you can make a fuss of both of them. If you take the baby out in the garden, let the pup come too.

If you are interested in some new object, you use your eyes. The pup will also do this, but his nose is more important to him. So let the puppy sniff the baby – that does not mean lick it all over – just allow the puppy to familiarise himself with the infant. If the puppy appears worried when the baby cries, try to ignore him or call him over and give him a treat. Never leave a puppy or a dog of any age alone with a baby or young child.

PUPPIES AND OTHER PETS

If you have a family cat who is used to dogs then, so long as you do not let the puppy chase it, everything should be OK. However, cats are unpredictable creatures and you cannot tell how a cat who is unaccustomed to dogs is going to react. Some will attack a small puppy such as a Yorkshire Terrier; others go berserk, climbing up the curtains and spitting furiously. Fortunately, most family cats are tolerant creatures – they have to be – and a little common sense should be all that is needed.

Your pup is almost certain to want to investigate this strange creature (unless he has been brought up with cats), so introduce them under controlled conditions in the house. Put the pup on a collar and lead, and if the cat just sits and stares, or bristles slightly, let the pup approach gradually, encouraging him in a normal voice. If the cat decides to take off, check the pup from chasing it, and try again. Never let the pup chase after the cat, yapping at her. Some cats will give a 'nosy' pup a hefty swipe with a paw. If the pup is large and bouncy, it will do him no harm and will probably make him more respectful next time. However, if you have a small puppy, try not to let this happen as it could scare him or even hurt him.

If you have pet rabbits or guinea pigs, they will probably be in hutches, cages or outside runs, so they should be safe from small puppies – but do not let the pup run round and round yapping at them. Introduce the puppy quietly, and check him with a harsh "No" if he refuses to leave them alone. Find something else for the puppy to do, play ball with him or give him a favourite toy. He should soon start accepting your small pets and lose interest, but never leave him alone with them.

A NEW PUPPY AND THE FAMILY DOG

Many people consider the idea of having a new puppy before the family dog becomes too old. In this way the loss of the older dog is often eased. However, think carefully before going ahead with this plan. Never bring in a young pup if you have a chronically sick, old dog, or one that suffers from arthritis or a similar joint illness. A stiff and creaky old granddad does not want small grandchildren crawling all over him – much as he may love them. The same goes for the old dog.

But if you have an old dog who enjoys the company of other dogs, one who has slowed down and mellowed, and perhaps lost some of his former drive, then a puppy may give him a new lease of life. We have seen a number of old dogs become like youngsters again when a lively, young puppy was introduced to the household. It is a matter of knowing your dog. If you feel that your dog would benefit from the company of a puppy – and the rest of the family want one – then go ahead and buy one.

When the puppy arrives home, introduce the pup and the old dog in the garden, where there is more space, and give them time to check each other over. You are, or should be, the pack leader, but the established dog will be dominant to the puppy – and the puppy will accept this. He is used to his mother being the boss dog and to taking his place in the litter with his siblings. So he will expect the older dog to boss him about, and so must you.

If, or more likely, when the old dog disciplines the puppy by turning him out of his bed, taking away a toy, giving a warning growl when he is eating, or a quick snap when he wants to be left alone to sleep, you must not interfere and take the puppy's part. Leave them to sort it out, and unless you are very unlucky, they will soon settle into a satisfactory relationship.

If you have children, you must explain to them that both dogs need equal attention. Despite the obvious temptations, the puppy must not be fussed over to

Big dogs are often gentle with small puppies – but they should not be left alone together, as the bigger dog could be unintentionally rough.

If you already have an established dog at home, make sure you do not make too much fuss of the puppy, making the older dog feel unloved. But in time, an older dog and a pup can become the best of friends.

It is important that your puppy learns the 'house rules' so that he knows what is allowed and what is considered unacceptable.

Consistency is all-important: do not allow your puppy to sit on the sofa on one occasion, and then tell him off the next time he does it.

the exclusion of the old dog. Again, you must emphasise that the children must not interfere if the old dog gives the puppy a telling-off. If they take the puppy's side, against the old dog, there will almost certainly be trouble.

Make sure that the two dogs are not together all the time. The old dog wants and deserves some peace in his old age, and the puppy will suffer from being with an older dog who he accepts as being the leader - especially if the old dog is a forceful character. The pup may play with him, sleep with him, give up his toys to him, even lie down when he does – but is likely to take very little notice of the rest of the family. He may grow up preferring the company of other dogs instead of learning to enjoy being with and working for the human members of the pack. You should be the most important influence in your puppy's life – not another dog.

So make sure your puppy spends some time alone, and some time alone with you or another member of the family. The pup should sleep alone, and if the dogs are left at home for a while, the puppy should be put in a crate, or in a different room. Take both dogs for walks and free runs together, but take the puppy to puppy classes on his own.

If you are sensible and allow the two dogs to sort themselves out, the puppy should soon become an integral part of the family. When the pup gets older and more mature, be prepared for him to take over as the dominant dog. Again, this is quite natural – it happens with humans too, when the son takes over the business from his father. So accept this, as the old dog may well be relieved that someone younger is taking over the responsibility of guarding the family!

PUPPIES AND CARS

Most dog owners like to take their dogs out with them, and there is no doubt that the sooner you start taking your pup in the car, the more likely he is to enjoy travelling. A young puppy is easier to control and less sensitive to his surroundings, and if he is sick there will be less mess to clear up! Many pups are good travellers from the start, but it must be admitted that quite a few suffer from car-sickness. If your puppy is prone to car-sickness, do not make the mistake of leaving him at home until he gets bigger. The chances are that he will be worse when he is older.

Sedatives or anti-sickness pills can often help; ask your vet to prescribe something suitable for your puppy's age and size. However, do not rely on using pills for every outing. It has been discovered that ginger is helpful in a lot of cases of travel sickness, in both humans and dogs. The best solution is to accustom your puppy to the car, and over a period of time he should become an excellent traveller.

You must decide where you want your puppy to travel in the car, bearing in mind that many dogs travel better when they cannot see out of the window. The pup can travel in a crate or a dog box if you wish. Or you can fix a screw-eye on the floor of an estate car or station wagon and hook the pup on to it with a short lead with a swivel. Some pups enjoy travelling in the passenger foot-well; this is not a bad place for a well-behaved dog – unless you have a passenger with large feet! Recently car seat belts for dogs have become available, although they would probably be more suitable for an older dog.

Personally, we do not like dogs behind dog-guards in a small space right at the back of the car. This area has not become known as the 'crumple zone' for nothing. It has the added disadvantage that you cannot reach the pup if he is worried, sick, or starts barking, and you can do nothing about it until you are able to stop the car and get out. This area can also get very hot for the dog. Before you start on a journey, make sure the pup has not been fed, and give him a chance to relieve himself. Put him on a collar and lead, and take along a friend (one who likes puppies, even messy ones) as a 'minder'. Make sure you are equipped with an old towel and some newspapers, just in case. If the pup is sick, do not make a fuss; clean him up, and as soon as you can, stop the car and let him out for a short run. This is often enough to settle a pup and he will be all right afterwards.

Make sure you keep the puppy quiet in the car. Nothing is worse than a dog who rushes back and forth, barking. If you have young children in the car, make it a rule that they do not play with the pup when travelling. It is a good idea to give him a toy or nylon bone to chew. Start with short trips and frequent stops. Try to go somewhere the puppy can run free, such as the local park. Let him out for a short run and then go on a little further and let him out again, perhaps on the way to a puppy class. Make the journeys fun; the puppy will not learn to enjoy the car if all he ever does is go to the shops or to the vet.

Once your puppy is happy about travelling, teach him to get in the car on his own – unless he is too small to jump in. Start with the pup sitting outside the door, get in the car yourself and then call him, encouraging him with a treat. Once the puppy is doing this, ask your puppy to sit, throw a treat into the car and tell him to "Get in". Praise him well when he responds. Never let your puppy get into the car until you say so, and never let him jump out until he is told. Get out of the car yourself, telling the pup to stay. If he tries to rush out, either push him back or hold him back with the lead. Wait until he has settled, then tell him "OK", and let him out, praising well. This is very important; dogs have been run over and caused accidents by jumping out of cars unexpectedly.

The final lesson is to teach your puppy to stay in the car on his own. If you have taught him to stay alone at home, this should not pose a problem. In fact, your problem is more likely to be with other people, children coming over to admire the "cute puppy", or holding their own dog up to the window to say hello – not to mention the ones who will come over and say "woof" in the hope that your puppy will answer them, as he undoubtedly will!

If you have a small puppy, it is best to leave him in a travelling box where he cannot be seen. When you first leave the pup, go a short distance away, just out of sight. If he does not bark after a minute or two, go back and praise him very well and give him a treat. If he does bark, go back and bang loudly on the roof of the car, growling "No". This nearly always works. Once the pup is quiet, leave him again and if he barks again, do the same thing. If he is quiet, go back and praise him. Only leave him for a very short time to begin with, and gradually increase it. You may have to work on this for quite a while, but it is well worth the effort to have a puppy who can be safely left on his own, knowing that he will behave. Just one last thought on cars. They can quickly turn into ovens, and many dogs have been literally cooked alive in cars. Even on a cool day the oxygen inside a car quickly gets used up. It is absolutely essential to have adequate ventilation in any static car with a dog inside. Do not forget that the sun moves, and although you may have parked your car in the shade, when you return two hours later, it could be in blazing sunshine.

HOUSE RULES

Start as you mean to go on. A friend of ours who trains dogs has a saying – 'Never

The first few weeks in a new home are a challenging time for a puppy.

Rest is an important part of development, and this Siberian Husky puppy appreciates some time when he is left undisturbed.

All puppies are inquisitive and will enjoy discovering the outside world.

However, puppies should get used to being tied up for short periods. This pup is quite happy to supervise the gardening.

sometimes.' As she says, it is a nonsensical phrase, but one that is well worth remembering.

An example would be the pup who rushes to welcome you home as you come through the door. He jumps all over you, licking and scrabbling, and you think: 'he really is fond of me now.' So you make a great fuss of him and tell him he is a good boy. But the next day, the children have been playing with the puppy in the garden; he rushes up to you with muddy paws and proceeds to jump all over you, confident that he is earning your pleasure. What will you do? The chances are that you will shout at him, telling him to get down, reprimanding him about how bad he is.

The puppy is left completely bewildered. All pups like to jump up; it is a natural action. They jump up at their mother to suckle, and they jump all over their siblings in play. So do not be too hard on your puppy when he jumps up at you – he means well. However, he must learn that this is unacceptable behaviour, especially if he is going to be a large adult! Sometimes it is enough to ignore your puppy when he jumps up, but make sure the rest of the family react in the same way. After a while, the pup should think it not worth jumping up if no one takes any notice.

However, most pups are persistent and you will have to do a bit more to stop this behaviour. Your object should be to teach the dog that you make a fuss of him when he is sitting – not when he is jumping up. In this instance, do not use the command "Down", as this should only mean 'lie down on the floor'. Instead, growl at your puppy (like his mother did when he was in the nest), push him down, and give the command "Sit". Once the puppy is sitting, praise him quietly. If you make too much fuss, he will start all over again.

Soon you should be able to tell your puppy to sit if you see he is about to jump up, and eventually he should abandon the idea. Do not allow your children to start shouting "Get down", "Stop it", etc., and flapping their hands about. This will just make your puppy over-excited, and will encourage him to bounce about even more. If you have not been firm enough with your puppy and he persists in jumping up, try holding his paws firmly, if he is a large puppy, until he climbs down.

When visitors come to the door, put your puppy on his lead and tell him to sit. Keep him in this position until the friend comes in. Ask the friend to gently stroke the puppy, and then let him free. If you want to impress your friends, teach your pup to shake hands. Most dogs (and visitors) enjoy this routine.

Another example of 'never sometimes' is if, when you are watching television, the pup creeps up beside you on the sofa. You think: 'well, he is rather cute', and let him stay. However, tomorrow Aunt Jane comes to visit, and she is not keen on dogs at the best of times. So when your puppy enthusiastically jumps on her lap, you shout at him, pull him off the sofa and shut him in the kitchen. In reality, it was *your* fault, not the pup's. So you must play fair and decide what your puppy can and cannot do. If he tries to come up on the sofa, and you have decided this is unacceptable, tell him "No", and send him to his own bed. Once he knows that is where he is meant to be, it will be easier for all of you. Try to stick to the rules, which is often easier said than done if you have children in the family. But it is well worth the effort when you are rewarded with a well-behaved dog, who knows what is expected of him without being told.

Once the puppy has learned his name, which he should always associate with pleasure, he must next learn "No" and "OK." No means 'stop what you are doing *now*'; and OK means just that. Do not shout at your puppy; he hears much better than you do. Growl out your 'No', and praise him in a happy voice.

Neither dogs nor puppies should go through doors or gates before you, or any other member of the family. The behaviourists emphasise that this is to show your dominance over the pup, but it also has a practical purpose. Puppies rushing through open doors can knock toddlers down, cause old people to fall, and trip up anyone in their way. A pup which rushes out of the door could run into the road and get knocked down by a car. So this is a useful rule for everyone's benefit.

When the situation first arises, simply say "No", and use your hand to hold the puppy back. Once you are through the door, tell him "OK", and pat him when he comes to you. As soon as you have taught your puppy to sit, tell him to sit before you open the door, and use a hand signal to help keep him there. Once you are through the door, tell him "OK", and call him. Do not make too much fuss of him or he will get over-excited. If your puppy is unsteady on his sit, put him on a lead until he is more reliable.

Although a pup should be left in peace to eat his food, he must be taught to accept the fact that you, or any of the family, have the right to go up to him when he is eating, or remove his food if you wish. Start off by telling your puppy to sit when you put down his food bowl, and then tell him he can eat. While he is eating, stroke him gently and talk to him. Most pups will be so busy eating, they will not even notice. But if your puppy does growl at you, immediately growl back, grasp him by the scruff of his neck and make him sit. Once he has calmed down, let him start eating again and stroke him. If your puppy is behaving well, drop a liver treat into his bowl to show him that you did not really want his dinner.

Keep repeating this at different times until your puppy accepts the stroking, then tell him to sit and remove his bowl. If he objects, treat him as before. When the puppy accepts this, take his bowl away and add some more food or a treat. In a short time most pups look forward to the bowl being removed and refilled with tasty bits.

If you have children, this lesson is very important. However often you remind them to leave the puppy alone, the day will come when one of them or a friend will run up when he is eating, bounce a ball near him, or make a grab at the food bowl. If the puppy has not been taught to accept having his food removed, there could be a nasty accident.

Young puppies use up an enormous amount of energy, so it is essential to feed a nutritious, well-balanced diet.

Chapter Four

CARING FOR YOUR PUPPY

FEEDING

DIETARY NEEDS

The dog is a carnivore, but long association with man means that his tastes are now omnivorous. Puppies have different needs from adult dogs. Young pups need three or four times the energy intake of an adult of the same breed. Not only do they need a basic maintenance allowance, but their energy intake must provide for activity and growth. Like human babies, puppies have small stomachs and therefore they need several small meals a day. At eight weeks, four meals a day are sufficient, gradually decreasing to one or two when adult. Small and Toy breeds mature early, usually around six to nine months, but large and giant breeds may not reach their adult weight until eighteen or even twenty-four months.

CHOOSING A DIET

As already stated, it is advisable to keep to the diet the pup is used to for the first few days. If you want to change the diet, do so gradually. There is a huge variety of puppy foods on the market, and those made by reputable firms are mostly very good. So you can take your pick from canned meat and/or dry food in a number of forms. What really matters is that the pup is fed a balanced diet, enjoys his food and thrives on it.

We always feed our puppies four meals a day: two meals of milk (or milk substitute) and cereal or puppy meal, and two meals of meat and puppy meal. At about three months we cut the puppies back to three meals, and then taper off to one meal a day when the dog is full-grown. We usually give our dogs a hard biscuit to go to bed with. This is a good idea with puppies as it gives them something to gnaw on, which is especially useful when they are teething. It helps to loosen the puppy teeth, it keeps the gums healthy, and the puppy is happily occupied for a while.

Recently there has been a trend of 'back to basics', with many breeders returning to the old-fashioned way of feeding, providing meat and biscuit. One advantage of this diet is that as puppies are fed a large amount of food for their size, and fed frequently, they tend to defecate a lot. Faeces from some complete diets can often be rather soft, and this seldom happens with a meat and biscuit diet.

Although a correctly balanced diet is the ideal, you will do no harm if you feed your puppy some 'human' foods. If you accustom your puppy to a variety of different foods and you are away from home and unable to obtain his usual diet, then he will be happy with an alternative. Baby cereals and milk substitutes are quite suitable for puppies, as are such things as milk puddings, finely chopped meat or baked brown bread. Eggs, cheese and fish are all good protein foods. The cost of feeding a dog has escalated in recent years and leftovers such as these can help the budget. Cooked eggs are more easily digested than raw eggs, but do not be put off feeding eggs because you have heard that raw egg-white is dangerous to dogs. Even one raw egg per day is very unlikely to be harmful.

SUPPLEMENTS

Do not be tempted by all the enticing advertisements for minerals, vitamins and other supplements – all guaranteed to make your puppy into everything you want him to be. If you are feeding a balanced diet, that is sufficient for your puppy's dietary needs. Extra minerals, etc. do more harm than good, particularly if you are feeding a 'complete' diet, which has been specially formulated to provide all the essential nutrients.

Dogs who are exercised in open country can pick up a surprising amount of natural nutrients which are not found in commercial dog foods. Grass, herbs, fruit (our dogs pick blackberries off the bushes), and even the odd helping of horse or sheep droppings are all beneficial. If your pup has limited access to such 'delicacies', the addition of a natural herbal/mineral supplement should help to keep him healthy.

WATER

A dog can go without food for several days, losing up to 40 per cent of his body weight without dying. However, with a water loss of ten to fifteen per cent, death can occur. Your puppy must have access to clean water all the time, especially if he is fed a dry diet. The exception to this is at night. You cannot expect a small pup to be dry at night if he has a large drink at 2am.

MEALTIMES

Wild dogs and wolves only eat when they manage to catch their dinner, and their puppies, once weaned, can only have a meal when some member of the pack brings it back – and that certainly is not four times a day! Most wildlife parks feed their canines three or four times a week as they remain much healthier fed that way. So do not feel that you must stick to exact feeding times or worry if your pup has to miss a meal for some reason or other. It will do the puppy no harm to wait a bit longer or have a meal a little earlier, if you find it necessary.

There is another advantage to varying feeding times. Puppies who are always fed 'on the dot' can develop into perfect pests when they grow up, demanding their dinner, come what may. Nothing is more aggravating than a dog who starts pestering and whining for his food at 11.45am when his feeding time is noon. So, start as you mean to go on and feed when you want to, not when the puppy asks for it.

Do not give the last meal too late at night. We feed this meal at about 8pm, which gives the pup time to digest his meal before bedtime, and also encourages him to be clean through the night. Never feed your puppy before taking him out in the car, nor before vigorous exercise. If you have a Toy breed and you are training with treats, remember that a handful of treats is probably as much as a whole meal to a tiny pup, so try to achieve a balance so that you are not over-feeding.

PROBLEM FEEDERS
Healthy puppies should be greedy puppies. If a healthy puppy says he does not want his dinner but begs you for something to eat, he is probably trying you out. Maybe he has smelled the chicken or salmon you were having for supper and fancies a bit. Do not give in to him. If your puppy leaves his food, just take the bowl away and offer him fresh food at the next mealtime. No healthy puppy has ever starved himself to death, and when your puppy realises that you are not going to offer him a series of different dishes to tempt his appetite, he will give in with good grace. However, if your pup refuses his food and appears to be off-colour, this is a cause for concern and you should consult your vet. Puppies need to be fit not fat, but we always like to see puppies well-covered. If a pup contracts a virus or stomach upset, he can lose weight alarmingly and will need some reserve to fall back on.

EXERCISE
All puppies – and all dogs of whatever age, size or breed – need exercise. They also need to play and very often the two can be happily combined. Young puppies should never be over-exercised, which means they should not be dragged on a lead for long walks or given too much free-running exercise. This applies to the giant breeds which mature more slowly than the Toy breeds. If you take your puppy with you when you go for a quiet ramble in the country or at the seaside, and allow him to go at his own pace, with frequent stops, he is unlikely to came to any harm.

Even young pups need exercise and play, which will help them to develop both physically and mentally. If you are taking your pup to 'puppy classes', he will get quite a lot of exercise and will learn social canine manners by playing with the other puppies. If you have a large garden or yard you can play games with your puppy there, or you can take him to the local park and other open spaces where dogs are allowed. Sensible exercise, which means never letting your puppy become really tired, can only do good. Never force a puppy to go on if he seems to be getting tired, and do not try to make him jump over awkward or high obstacles until he is at least six or even nine months old.

If you live near the sea, a river or lake and you have a gundog pup, such as a Labrador Retriever, you will probably have trouble keeping him out of the water. But many other breeds love swimming too. If your pup is a natural swimmer, you must still be very careful not to let him go out too far, and do not throw anything for him to retrieve in a fast-flowing river or a rough sea.

Some pups need a bit of coaxing to get them started in the water. If your pup is this sort, do not be in a hurry – and never attempt to throw him in. The best way is to go in yourself and call the pup in with you. If you have a small breed, you will probably get away with paddling. But if you have a large dog who is a reluctant swimmer, then you will just have to go swimming yourself – and hope he does not sit on the shore watching you! To persuade the pup to go in the water, toss something for him to retrieve, have a tug-of-war with a bit of rope – any sort of game to persuade him that this is fun. However, do not over-tire a youngster.

GROOMING
All dogs, from an Irish Wolfhound to a Chihuahua need grooming, but it is also an

It is a good idea to get your puppy used to being groomed from an early age. This Borzoi puppy looks big, but he is only nine weeks old.

This Golden Retriever puppy is quite happy to be groomed on the table.

The long-coated Afghan needs an increasing amount of attention as the coat grows.

important part of canine life. Wild dogs groom each other in an act of friendship, and this helps to cement the whole pack together. In a domestic situation, the grooming session should always be something for the pup to enjoy; it should never become a battlefield. If it is properly carried out, grooming strengthens the bond between puppy and owner.

Few puppies need much grooming, and if you have a short-coated breed, such as a Whippet, you may feel it is not worth bothering. This is definitely not the case. All puppies need to be handled, and you cannot start too soon. It will be time well spent, and a vet or judge will appreciate a dog who behaves sensibly and allows itself to be handled without any fuss. Most puppies love being talked to and petted. When you have a spare moment, pick the pup up and sit with him on your lap. If you have a large puppy, just sit on the floor with him. Quietly coax the pup to sit still while you run your hands over him, open his mouth, pick up his feet, look in his ears – rub his tummy if you like; the object of the exercise is for the puppy to enjoy the experience. If your puppy wriggles, keep a firm hold on him until he relaxes, then praise him or give him a treat and finish for the day.

Once the puppy accepts being handled, place him on a table, and start brushing him, making sure you use a good-quality bristle brush. The pup can be sitting, standing or lying down. If you have a long-coated breed, grooming is easier if the dog learns to lie flat. If the pup already knows to lie down, give him a command such as "Flat", and gently roll him on his side, keeping him there for a few seconds. Once the puppy is relaxed, praise him and let him get up again. Be firm, but do not have a fight. As soon as your puppy is lying quietly, you can start brushing him.

Most breeds only need a few minutes grooming daily, and a thorough grooming once a week. That is, unless you have an Old English Sheepdog, an Afghan Hound, or a Pekingese. If this is the case, then we hope you like grooming, as you will have to spend a lot of time doing it!

TYPES OF COAT

SMOOTH-COATED: If you have a smooth-coated breed, a hound glove is very useful. These usually have short, rubber teeth on one side, and corduroy or velvet on the other side. The rubber side is excellent for removing dead hairs, and the other side is for massaging and 'polishing'. You can always use your hands to massage your dog, and this is something which most dogs love. The purpose of this is to stimulate the blood supply to the skin and hair follicles, and to tone up the muscles.

LONG-COATED: A long-coated dog is more likely to develop mats and tangles in his coat. Gently comb out the hair, using a steel comb, and check behind the ears and under the armpits, where mats are very likely to form. Combs should always be used carefully; they are not for tugging out chunks of hair, although they are often used for this. Any knots or tangles should be gently teased out. Brush a small amount of coat at a time, making sure the bristles go right down to the skin and working over the whole animal.

WIRE-HAIRED: Wire-haired dogs, like Wire Fox Terriers, have harsh outer coats and dense, soft undercoats which will need regular 'stripping.' This is usually done with a 'stripping knife', which looks rather like a penknife with serrated edges. All the Terrier breeds are trimmed in different styles, and so if you aim to show your puppy, you will need to seek professional help. If you just want to keep your pup as a companion, then you could learn to trim him yourself. Ask the breeder for advice or buy a book on the breed. In between trims, this type of coat should only need regular brushing.

STIFF/STAND-OFF: Breeds with stiff, stand-off coats, such as some of the Spitz breeds, Chow Chows, Keeshonds, etc. should first have their coats brushed against the growth of the hair and then carefully brushed back into place. When these breeds shed their coat, the amount of hair that comes out is unbelievable! A special rake can help to remove this more easily.

NON-SHEDDING: Poodles, and a few other breeds, do not shed their coats – which is a great help to any dog-lover who suffers from asthma. This type of coat keeps on growing, and unless it is properly looked after it can end up in a matted mess. Most Poodle owners use the services of a grooming parlour on a regular basis, although you can learn to do it yourself. There are several short grooming courses available if you wish to do this.

Whatever type of pup you have, always keep your grooming equipment clean; it is not much use grooming a dog with a dirty brush.

NAILS

In the wild, canines wear their nails down naturally, as do most stray dogs who roam around in urban areas. However, most dogs kept as companions will need to have their nails cut and/or filed regularly. Some pups are very sensitive about their feet, so start handling feet very early on. Make a game of it, rolling the pup over, catching hold of his feet and playing with him. When the puppy accepts this, you can progress until the pup will lie still and allow you to examine his feet. Do not forget to reward the puppy when he does what you want.

When a dog is standing naturally, his nails should just touch the ground. If the nails are too long it makes walking very uncomfortable. The nails tend to split and often the feet splay out. Another disadvantage of long nails – for you, not the pup – is that long nails can hurt, especially sharp puppy nails! To begin with, your puppy's nails may not need much attention, but it is a good practice to keep the tips snipped off. Once the nails are allowed to grow too long, it is a difficult job to get them right again.

Buy some strong, good-quality nail-clippers. There are many different types to choose from, so just pick the type you prefer. A coarse file can be used to smooth off rough edges. If your pup really hates having his nails cut – and this should not be the case if you have handled him properly – you may find that he tolerates a nail-file quite happily.

Light-coloured nails are much easier to clip than dark ones, because the quick, showing as a thin, pink line down the middle of the nail, is easily seen. Be very careful never to cut the quick; it is extremely painful, it bleeds profusely, and it can put a puppy off having his nails cut.

The smooth-coated Boxer is easy to care for. A hound glove is a useful item of equipment for this type of coat.

Like many of the terrier breeds, the Border Terrier has a harsh, dense coat.

The Poodle does not shed its coat, and most owners enlist the services of a grooming parlour in order to keep the coat in shape.

It is a good idea to get your puppy used to being bathed at an early age.

If your puppy has both light and dark nails, cut the light ones first. This will give you a better idea of how much to take off the dark nails, where you cannot see the quick. If in doubt, it is usually safe to trim off the tip of the nail at the point where it starts to turn down. It is often easier to see where to cut a nail by turning the foot up and cutting from underneath the pad.

If your puppy has dewclaws (usually located on the inside of the front legs, occasionally on the inside of back legs too), these must be checked regularly. Obviously they do not come into contact with the ground, so they just keep on growing. If neglected, they can grow right into the leg, causing a nasty abscess and a lot of unnecessary pain.

TEETH

When you first have your puppy he should have a set of twenty-eight 'baby' teeth, which, as you will soon discover, are unpleasantly sharp! Between four and seven months, the permanent teeth (averaging forty-two in number) will start coming through, first the incisors and lastly the molars. Unlike human babies, puppies rarely have teething troubles, but teething can cause a certain amount of stress, and puppies often become more sensitive to their environment during the teething period.

At this time be careful how you handle your pup, especially round his mouth. For instance, do not start trying to teach him to retrieve by forcing a hard dumb-bell in his mouth! When a puppy is teething, he *must* chew; it is part of the teething process. The puppy will chew to loosen his baby teeth which must make way for the adult teeth. You must therefore make sure that your puppy has plenty of hard, nylon or rubber toys he can have a go at.

In most cases, the baby teeth come out on their own, but in some of the smaller breeds, especially Toys, they are retained as the new ones come in. Keep an eye on this, as if left too long, the correct placement of the permanent teeth can be affected. Keep checking to see if the teeth are coming loose, and if they do not appear to be moving, consult your vet, as they may need to be extracted.

Most dogs, like most people, develop tartar on their teeth – although this is unlikely to happen with a puppy or young dog. If you keep the teeth in good condition while the dog is still young, it can help to prevent tartar forming. There are several things you can do to help. Make sure the pup has something hard to chew on even if he has finished teething. Hard nylon toys, good-quality rubber toys, hard biscuits and marrow bones are all suitable.

Most vets now advise cleaning a dog's teeth about once a week. There are various 'doggy' toothpastes and toothbrushes on sale. But you can do a good job with a gauze pad soaked in saline solution or soda bicarbonate and water. Rub this round the teeth vigorously, or use an ordinary toothbrush if you wish. The inner surfaces of the teeth are usually kept clean by the action of the dog's tongue. Never throw stones for a dog to retrieve. Not only might he swallow one, but he could easily chip or break his teeth playing with them.

BATHING

It always surprises us that the majority of breed books insist that a dog should never be bathed unless absolutely necessary – i.e. if he has rolled in something disgusting! However, nobody likes living with a dirty dog, and we have always found that a good bath freshens a dog up, makes for a healthy coat and certainly makes him more pleasant to live with. Very young puppies should not need bathing, but if it is necessary, it is vital that the puppy is well dried off and not allowed to become cold.

Even though your pup may not need a bath, it is a good idea to get him used to it while he is still fairly young – and manageable! If possible, choose a dry, sunny day. If you suspect your puppy has fleas, you will need to use an insecticidal shampoo. If this is not the case, it is advisable to buy a good-quality dog shampoo. Never attempt to use the washing-up detergent or your own shampoo.

Depending on the size of your puppy you can use the sink, the shower, or a tub, but do not fill it. Make sure the surface is not slippery; if the pup starts sliding about on a slippery surface he could hate bathtime for ever more. The water should be warm, and should come up no higher than the puppy's tummy. Lift the pup carefully into the water, and wet him thoroughlu with a sprayer attachment before you apply shampoo, working it into a good lather. Leave the puppy's head until last. Once his head is wet he will want to shake, and you will be left soaking wet with the pup only half-washed. Be careful not to get shampoo into his eyes or ears. If you are worried about the ears, put some cotton-wool (cotton) in them; the puppy may shake it straight out but it could help.

Once your puppy is really clean, rinse him thoroughly by pouring tepid water over him. If you have a shower attachment, that will make the job easier. Do not rinse in hot water; this will make the puppy feel cold afterwards. When you are satisfied that you have rinsed out all the shampoo, slip a lead on your puppy, lift him out of the water and let him have a good shake. Do not let the pup loose to run around – it can be guaranteed that he will roll in something nasty, if he can find it, and you will have to start all over again. Give the puppy a good rub with a rough towel, and either take him for a walk if it is a sunny day, or take him to play on the lawn.

If your pup is a long-coated breed such as an Afghan Hound, a Rough Collie, or a Bearded Collie, it is better to dry him with a hair-dryer. If you attempt to dry this type of coat with a towel the hair may tangle or break. If you are going to use a hair-dryer, get the pup used to it before you actually need to dry him. This is best achieved by having the puppy lie on the floor or your lap (depending on size), while you talk to him and play with one of his toys in one hand. Hold the dryer in your other hand and put it on at a low setting, gradually bring it nearer the puppy until he accepts it. If you take your time, the puppy will learn to enjoy the experience.

When you are bathing your puppy, try to make it fun. Never fight with a struggling pup and make a big issue of it. Approached with common sense, bath time can be pleasant for you and your dog.

A number of preventative health programmes should be followed in order to keep your dog fit and healthy.

Inoculation programmes should start in puppyhood and be continued with annual boosters throughout your dog's life.

Chapter Five

HEALTH MATTERS

In the first twelve months of life, hopefully, your puppy will experience minimal health problems. However, there are a number of preventative health programmes that should be adopted, and you, as the owner, must keep a check on any other problems which may arise.

WEEKLY CHECKS
Once a week you should give your puppy a thorough grooming and check-up. Start at the head, looking at the eyes which should be bright and clear. Dogs with protruding or deep-set eyes can sometimes get sore eyes from dust or sand blowing into them. You can help this by washing the eyes out with normal saline solution: a teaspoonful of salt added to a quart of boiled water, and allowed to cool. Apart from this simple bathing procedure, never attempt to treat any other eye problems. Eyes are very delicate and can easily be harmed, so always take the puppy to the vet for treatment.

Next check the nose, which should be clear and free from discharge. In very dry, hot weather or in severe cold weather, the nose can sometimes become sore or cracked. If your dog tends to use his nose as a digging tool, the skin may become a little raw. If this is the case, a smear of olive oil, petroleum jelly or cod liver oil will help. The puppy will lick most of it off, but what is left will do some good.

Next open the mouth and check the teeth and gums. Gums should be healthy and pink in colour, although some breeds have black or black-spotted gums. Once your puppy starts teething, check the mouth quite frequently to make sure the second teeth are coming in correctly. Lastly check the ears. Never poke anything into an ear. If the ear is foul-smelling or has an unpleasant discharge, seek veterinary advice. However, you can easily clean off any normal dirt or wax with damp cotton-wool (cotton). Wrap it around your finger and rub the dirt off, as you will do no harm this way. In the summer watch out for grass-seeds which can cause problems in breeds with long, silky-coated ears, such as spaniels.

Now work down to the feet, checking the pads for any cuts or cracks, and looking to see if the nails need to be trimmed. Look between and under the pads: some long-haired breeds tend to get mats in between the toes. If these are not cut out they can cause lameness and sore feet. The best way to do this is with a pair of blunt-nosed, curved scissors.

If you have a male puppy, check the penis and sheath. In a puppy or young dog any slight discharge should be light and clear. If there is a smelly or discoloured discharge you should consult your vet. Most male dogs leave drops of urine scattered around underneath when they urinate. In long-haired breeds this tends to make the hairs round the sheath sticky and rather unpleasant. So it is advisable to keep the hair short in this area and give it an occasional wash.

VACCINATION

Puppies are now usually vaccinated against distemper, leptospirosis, hepatitis and parvovirus. In some countries where rabies is endemic it is usually compulsory for dogs to be vaccinated against this disease. Dogs do not usually contract tetanus, but it can happen, usually in country districts. If you live in a 'tetanus-prone' area, it is worth asking your vet for advice.

Many vets are unwilling to vaccinate a puppy before it is twelve weeks old, giving the second vaccination at sixteen weeks, although this may vary from area to area. It is advised that the puppy is not taken out beyond the garden until the inoculation programme is complete. However, in Britain, the Guide Dogs for the Blind Association has operated a policy of vaccinating all puppies at six weeks of age, completing the programme at around three months. The reason for this is that puppies who are isolated in the house and garden between six and twelve weeks miss out on a vital period of socialisation, at a time when they are at their most receptive. The GDBA has operated this policy for some twenty-five years and literally thousands of puppies have suffered no ill-effects. For many years now we have always had our pups vaccinated at six weeks, and there have been no resulting health problems.

No one is suggesting that you take the pup to the nearest park and put him down by the nearest lamp-post used by all and sundry! But if you are sensible and take him to clean areas in the country, to friends who have healthy dogs or puppies, and around town in the car, he will have every chance of growing up into a normal, well-socialised, happy dog. Obviously, you must decide which inoculation programme you wish to pursue. In a very few breeds, such as Irish Wolfhounds, puppies can be adversely affected when vaccinated at twelve to fourteen weeks, as it appears to affect their immune system. This is very rare, and the breeder will almost certainly have given you advance warning. If you have been warned, make sure your vet is aware of the situation. Your puppy may have had his first injection before leaving the breeder, in which case he will have to go to the vet to finish the course. After the course is finished, your dog will need boosters, probably annually, but it will depend on the incidence of infectious diseases in your locality. Once again, your vet will be able to advise you.

INTERNAL PARASITES

ROUNDWORMS

No one's favourite subject, but one which, as a dog owner, you cannot avoid! At one time or another your dog – and everyone else's dog – will have worms. This is nothing to be alarmed about, but you must obviously adopt a programme of worming treatment starting when your puppy first arrives home and continuing throughout his life. Virtually all puppies have roundworms called Toxocara Canis. Although pups can have worms without any tell-tale signs in their faeces, roundworms can often be seen as whitish-coloured thread-like objects, usually from 2-8ins (5-20cms) long. Toxocara Canis *can* cause blindness in humans, but it very seldom *does*. In twenty years, no case of complete blindness caused by Toxocara Canis has been recorded at Moorfields, the largest eye hospital in Britain. If your puppy is wormed regularly there will be no danger to you, your family or the general public.

Most vets recommend worming for roundworms in puppies at two, four, six, eight and twelve weeks. There are innumerable remedies available on the market. Many of these can be fed to the puppy with his normal meal. In fact, some wormers are now incorporated into the food. Most are easy to administer and produce little, if any, adverse reaction. Although many worming products can be bought 'over the counter', it is advisable to ask your vet for advice to ensure you have a safe, effective remedy. Your vet can also advise on a future worming programme for when your puppy is older. In most cases, dogs should be wormed routinely every six months, and at any other time the owner suspects their dog may be infested.

There are other worms which affect dogs, tapeworms being the most common. Heartworms can affect dogs living in some parts of the USA. Your vet can test your puppy and put him on a preventative.

EXTERNAL PARASITES

FLEAS
The best-cared-for puppy can pick up fleas, especially if he comes into regular contact with other dogs. It is also more of a problem in the warm weather. Regular grooming will help to keep your dog free from fleas, but you will also need to use some other preventative measure. There are a number of anti-parasitic flea sprays available which are very effective. These should be used on a once-weekly basis. You may prefer to use a flea collar. These usually have to be renewed every three months – they should not be used in conjunction with a flea spray.

If your puppy is scratching, look for evidence of flea infestation. You may not see the fleas themselves, but you will probably see evidence in the form of 'flea-dirt' – black grain-like droppings. The most effective solution is to bathe your puppy, using an insecticidal shampoo. Remember that fleas can live in carpets and on bedding, so you must spray areas where your puppy lies, and wash all bedding thoroughly.

TICKS
If you live in sheep or deer-grazing areas, your puppy may pick up a tick. These parasites suck at the dog's blood until they become bloated. Do not be tempted to try to pull the tick from your puppy, as this will leave the mouth-piece firmly implanted in the dog's skin. The best treatment is to apply some cotton-wool (cotton), soaked in a mild antiseptic, and the tick will release its hold.

DIARRHOEA
The most common problem a puppy is likely to suffer in the first twelve months of its life is diarrhoea, caused by an upset stomach. There may be many reasons for this. The puppy may have eaten too much; he may have reacted to a change of diet, or he may have picked up a bug. If your puppy is suffering from diarrhoea, the best course of action is to withhold food for a twenty-four period making sure that fresh, clean drinking water is readily available. When you next feed your puppy, give him something plain and easy to digest such as chicken or fish and rice. In most

A good diet, with hard biscuits to chew on, will ensure that your puppy's teeth are free from tartar.

Your puppy should be checked over once a week to ensure that any problems are caught at the earliest stage.

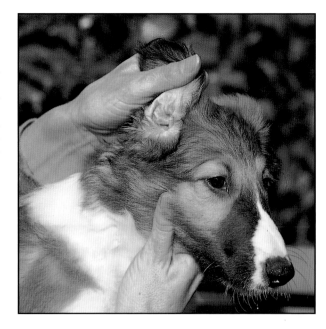

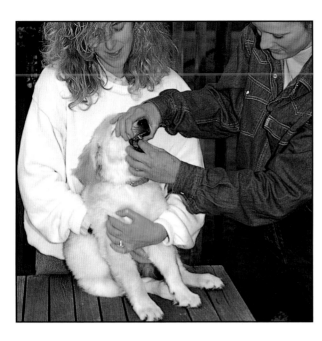

It is important to practise giving your dog a tablet – by using a treat – so that you do not have a battle when you need to dose a sick dog.

A syringe (without the needle) is very useful for giving liquid medicine. To begin with, you will need to enlist the help of a friend to make sure that the puppy does not struggle or become upset.

cases this will solve the problem. However, if the condition persists, ask your vet for advice. If, at any time, you see signs of blood in the stools, contact your vet immediately.

GIVING MEDICATION

PILLS

Sooner or later your puppy will need to be dosed, even if he only needs a worm pill. There is only one way to make sure that he has the right dose, and that is to put the pill down his throat. If you put it in his food he may leave it; if you break it up in his food he may leave all of it or only eat half of it. Additionally, there are some drugs with special coverings which do not release the contents until they reach that part of the gut where they are best absorbed.

The last thing you want with a sick dog, or a healthy one for that matter, is to have a fight when trying to dose him as it will only cause more stress. So make sure your puppy is used to being dosed before it becomes a necessity. Start with a substitute, like chocolate drops or liver treats, and offer the pup one or two to eat. Then place your hand over his muzzle, lift his head slightly and holding the lips down over the top teeth, gently press inwards. Keep the upper lips between the fingers and teeth. This should cause the pup to open his mouth, and then you can quickly pop a treat inside and praise him well.

After doing this a couple of times, place the next treat as far back on the tongue as possible. Once the puppy accepts this, alternate giving him a treat to take on his own with putting one in his mouth. When it comes to dosing your puppy with a pill, he should tolerate the procedure without any fuss. If your pup is very small – or you have very large hands – you may have to aim the pill to the back of the tongue and drop it. Otherwise, place it as far back as you can, shut the pup's mouth, keep the head tilted slightly upwards and massage the throat. If a dog is reluctant to swallow, this often helps. Always make sure the pill is placed really well back – dogs are expert at spitting out pills!

LIQUID MEDICINE

The easiest way to give liquid medicine is with a syringe or small plastic bottle. Get the pup to sit, and gently insert a finger at the side of the mouth, between the teeth and cheek. Pull the lips outwards to form a pouch, keeping the head tilted slightly upwards. Place the loaded syringe in the mouth and gently squeeze (or pour if using a bottle) the liquid in. Only place as much liquid as the pup can easily swallow at one time. Never squirt in a large dose as you will make him choke.

If you can get someone to hold the pup when you first start this procedure, it will make it easier for you and your dog. Make sure that you use something tasty such as milk or gravy. If the pup does not swallow immediately, massage his throat while keeping the head slightly tilted, and this will usually help the medicine go down.

Chapter Six

UNDERSTANDING YOUR PUP

THE DOG'S MIND

"He understands every word I say to him" is an often-heard remark. But dogs do not understand any words at all as we understand them. It is just as easy to teach a dog to lie down by saying "Stand up", as by saying "Lie down." Dogs understand sounds, and they are more responsive than we are to different sounds. They are also far more responsive to body language and facial expression, which sometimes gives rise to the belief that they are telepathic. "He knows when I am in a bad mood", says the fond owner. Of course he knows when you are in a bad mood! Don't all the other members of your family know when you are in a bad mood without being told?

There is some difference of opinion as to whether dogs reason as we do. The scientific school of thought is that a dog does not work out how to solve a problem, he only thinks about what he is doing at any given time. However, many dog owners would claim that they have seen examples of dogs working out problems for themselves – usually to their own advantage! It is difficult to be absolutely certain whether a dog has solved a problem, or whether this has happened by chance or in response to an instinct. It is very unwise to assume that a dog is reasoning, and the possibility of your young puppy reasoning is virtually non-existent.

ASSOCIATION OF IDEAS

Dogs learn by association of ideas, as do all the higher animals. This simply means that if an animal does something either accidentally or by persuasion and finds it pleasant, he will tend to do it again. If it is unpleasant, he will be reluctant to do it again. We associate certain sights and sounds and smells with pleasant or unpleasant experiences. A child can be told that touching the fire will be very painful, and if he understands the spoken language, he is unlikely to try it out. But the child who is not yet talking will not understand and may well put a finger in the fire – though he is very unlikely to do it again! In fact, he may well be terrified of going anywhere near the fire for a very long time.

Frightening experiences give rise to the strongest and most permanent associations of ideas. To many people, the screech of tyres brings vivid memories of terror or tragedy, or it could be the sight of a certain spot by the roadside which brings back similar memories to someone else. The same sight or sound could have different associations for different people. A tune which provides very pleasant memories for one person may bring equally unpleasant memories for someone else. We believe that the association of ideas affects dogs in exactly the same way as it

Dogs learn by association of ideas, and this is reinforced in training by a system of correction and reward. It is important to gain the dog's attention when training and to hold it for as long as possible.

The Border Collie usually has an exceptionally strong herding instinct, which is an asset to the shepherd but may be a liability to the pet owner.

The retriever breeds, such as the Labrador Retriever and the Golden Retriever have been bred as superb gundogs. Most puppies will pick up any object and carry it around without any encouragement or training.

affects humans – but it is surprising how many dog owners have difficulty understanding that simple fact.

CORRECTION AND REWARD

In order to get the dog to do what we want, and just as important, to refrain from doing what we do not want, we build up desirable association of ideas by a process of correction and reward. Correction could be described as any action which prevents the dog doing what he intends, or persuades him to do what the trainer wants him to do – such as pushing him into a sitting position.

Only the minimum of correction should ever be used, and when the dog responds, no matter how reluctantly, he should be *immediately* rewarded. It is easy to over-correct, but it is very difficult to over-reward. To be effective it is essential that correction or reward is applied as the action takes place, or within seconds of it taking place. The vast majority of behavioural problems can be attributed to the owner's failure to exploit timing.

STRENGTH OF ASSOCIATIONS

As has already been pointed out, the strongest and most lasting associations are those created by fear. Following this are the first-time associations, and experiences which happen over and over again. If a puppy is frightened by the first dog he meets, the effect will be far greater than if he had previously met friendly dogs. This is well-known among dog show exhibitors. A puppy who has a bad fright at his first show, for whatever reason, may be put off showing for life. But if he gets a fright after going to several shows, which he has enjoyed, the effect will be much less. And, of course, the effect will be greater if he has a nasty experience at several shows in succession.

Another point to remember is that the effect of frightening experiences increases as the puppy gets older. A sixteen-week-old puppy may be absolutely terrified of something which would not have affected him at all when he was seven weeks.

A threatened animal can adopt one of three options: fight, flight or freeze. Many dogs have been turned into fighters by being attacked when they were adolescents. However, it is rare for a young puppy to fight, no matter the provocation. The pup will either freeze by becoming submissive – probably rolling on his back and waving his paws in the air; or he will flee, which is the biggest danger of all. First, there is the very real danger that the puppy might run into the path of an oncoming car. But that is not the only danger.

The instant the puppy bolts, he has separated himself from his protector, and the further he runs the greater does the separation become, with the puppy becoming even more terrified. So much so that by the time the pursuer decides to give up the chase, the puppy is completely disorientated. Like a lost child, he panics and becomes even more terrified. It is difficult to imagine anything more frightening, and one experience of this sort has left many a bold, friendly puppy terrified of strange dogs for life.

Like all experiences, this one can create different associations. The most likely is that the puppy will be afraid of strange dogs, or he may only be afraid of the type of dog which frightened him. We have a Chihuahua who was frightened by a black dog, and years later is still afraid of black dogs – but he is not frightened of dogs of any other colour. Additionally, the puppy may associate the fright with the place, and he may be afraid of going near the spot where the incident took place, even when there is no dog there. If the puppy gets chased by a dog, or dogs on several occasions – which we hope will not happen – he may be apprehensive about going out for a walk at all.

RELATING TO OTHER DOGS
It goes against the laws of nature for an adult dog to attack a submissive puppy, and it is very rare to find one that does. But it is natural for any dog to chase anything which runs away, be it a child, a sheep, a puppy, or a ball rolled along the ground. When you take your puppy out in a public, open space, you should always assume that the dogs you meet are *not under control*. Most of them will be, but a false assumption can lead to big trouble.

If a strange dog comes bounding up, do not worry about whether or not he is friendly, and certainly do not listen to the owner's assurance to that effect. Just make sure your puppy does not flee by putting him on a lead when you see the dog approaching. Do not drag the pup away from the other dog; do not scream at him "Come here", and do not pick him up. In short, do not do anything that might give the impression that there is anything to be frightened of.

When they are afraid, some puppies will run to their owners for protection. That is the sort we like. Others are braver and stand their ground until the last minute, then lose their nerve and take off towards the horizon. If the strange dog proves to be friendly, allow him to sniff the puppy, but do not touch either of them, and do not offer the puppy tidbits while the interaction is taking place.

Puppy classes, where your puppy can meet other youngsters in a controlled environment before going out into the big wide world, can be a great help. The puppies taking part vary enormously in every way, including temperament: some are bouncy, playful extroverts, others are shy introverts. By being allowed – never forced – to mix, the nervous pup will learn that the bold, confident pup only wants to play and has no intention of attacking, and the bouncy pup is taught not to go tearing after every pup he sees.

At puppy classes, puppies also learn to mix with strangers, both adults and children, and to discover that this can be fun, usually ending with a tasty treat. But above all the puppy learns the body language of his kind, which teaches him how to behave in the accepted manner with strange dogs, how to react to different dogs in different situations, and, above all, never to run away when he sees a strange dog.

INSTINCT AND INTELLIGENCE
It is doubtful whether anything causes so much confusion in the minds of dog owners as the relationship between instinct and intelligence. To the vast majority of owners, the outstanding feature of any dog, especially their own, is his intelligence. But, in fact, the reason why the dog has become such a valuable servant and friend to mankind is because of his instincts. Most dogs are sufficiently intelligent to be able to learn anything we want to teach them, provided the right instincts are there.

Both instinct and intelligence can be an asset or a liability. The submissive dog is likely to use his intelligence in order to understand the wishes of the owner. The dominant dog is just as likely to use his intelligence to find ways of evading his owner's wishes. We spent many years training, or re-training, so-called difficult and disobedient dogs, belonging to other people. Virtually all of these dogs were very

Sighthounds, such as this Greyhound, Afghan Hounds and Salukis, have a highly developed chasing instinct. This has to be controlled in a domestic situation.

The terrier breeds, which include the Staffordshire Bull Terrier, are tough, active, and full of character.

The German Shepherd Dog, one of the guarding breeds, is used as a police dog worldwide. However, in police-work today the hunting instinct, used for tracking, is becoming increasingly important.

intelligent – often more so than their owners, which was usually the cause of the problem!

Instinct makes an animal do something without any learning. The first instinct to make an appearance is the instinct to survive, which makes the newborn puppy squirm around until he finds a teat and then start sucking. As he grows up, other instincts will develop. These will vary according to the breed, and they will also vary in strength between individuals of the same breed.

All breeds have inherited some hunting instinct from the wolf. By careful selective breeding, man has strengthened this instinct in some breeds until it is stronger than in its wild ancestor. The wolf only hunts when it is hungry, but many breeds of dog will hunt just for the sake of hunting. Man has also modified the hunting instinct to develop instincts which he can use to his own advantage. The best examples of these are the herding and retrieving instincts.

THE HERDING INSTINCT

The herding instinct in the modern Border Collie is an example of the extent to which man can develop an instinct for his own purpose. Contrary to common belief, it is not because of its superior intelligence that the Border Collie reigns supreme in sheepdog trials – it is because of the breed's instinct to herd. The average Labrador Retriever is just as intelligent as the average Border Collie, but a Labrador will not work sheep because it has no herding instinct. However, the Labrador will usually retrieve instinctively, and although most breeds will retrieve, in most cases they have to be taught, whereas the Labrador just does it instinctively.

The herding instinct in the modern Border Collie is often over-developed to the extent that many of the breed are obsessed with working. This is a good example of how an instinct which can be an asset to one owner, can be a liability to another. To anyone wanting to compete in sheepdog trials, the herding instinct in his dog cannot be too strong. But that sort of dog will herd anything from the neighbour's cat to a double-decker bus, which can obviously lead to trouble!

This exceptionally strong herding instinct is very often accompanied by an abundance of initiative and energy. We therefore have a dog that can be taught to do virtually anything that a dog can be expected to do, but if given nothing to do, will become so frustrated as to become mentally deranged.

Puppies begin to show their instincts at various ages. Sheepdog puppies often want to work at eight weeks when they are far too young to be allowed to do so. In contrast, we have known of several sheepdogs who showed no interest in work until they were a year old or more, and still turned out to be very good workers. Instincts strengthen with use. If encouraged, a sheepdog puppy who shows a mild interest today is likely to be a lot keener tomorrow, and even more keen the next day. This is totally at odds with those who think that if their Border Collie is trained to work, he will be less likely to chase sheep. The reverse is more likely to be the case.

If a pup is not allowed to use an instinct, that instinct will usually become weaker and perhaps die out completely. A sheepdog puppy who is prevented from working when the instinct is developing, may refuse to take any interest in sheep by the time he is a year old. However, he may well have become 'hooked' on something else like horses, cars, boys on bikes, etc. If you want a dog to work, start him when he wants to 'run'. If you do not want him to work, do not let him start – find something else into which he can channel his energy.

THE RETRIEVING INSTINCT

Other breeds have instincts which have been developed by man for various purposes, and this includes the retrievers (which include several different breeds) and most spaniel breeds. Dogs of this breeding will usually pick up objects and carry them around without any training or encouragement, although the age at which they start showing this instinct can vary between individuals. One puppy may show a strong retrieving instinct at six weeks, while his litter-brother may not show any inclination to retrieve until he is five months or older.

All dogs enjoy having something to do: a very large number of dogs get into trouble because they are unemployed. One way to overcome this is to make use of the instincts which your particular type of dog has inherited. If you have a spaniel or retriever pup, encourage him to bring your slippers, pick up the mail, carry a parcel when out shopping, etc. Or you might like to take your dog to pick up at a local shoot, or enter him for gundog tests. Whatever you decide to do, he will be far happier using his instincts than sitting idly at home in the garden – or worse, digging it up through frustration.

THE HUNTING INSTINCT

Hound puppies frequently have an even stronger hunting instinct than the wild dog. They can be divided into two groups: sighthounds who hunt by sight, and scenthounds who hunt by using their noses. Sighthounds include such breeds as Afghans, Salukis, Greyhounds and Whippets. They disprove the commonly-held belief that dogs have poor eyesight compared with humans. A Greyhound will spot a moving hare half a mile away, before the average human can see it. There is organised racing in which most sighthounds can take part – you can usually get particulars from the breed clubs. There is also organised racing specifically for Greyhounds and for Whippets. Scenthounds do not bother to look – they simply put their noses down and follow the track of their quarry. This is something which we 'superior' humans cannot do and despite extensive research, we still do not know how the dog does it! Beagles and Basset Hounds, both popular as pets, are well-known members of this group. There are official packs of Beagles, Bassets and Bloodhounds, but the Breed clubs often have small packs where owners of pet hounds can go along and enjoy a day of sport.

THE GUARDING INSTINCT

The guarding instinct probably affects more dog owners than any other instinct. Most people like to think that their dog would protect them if the occasion arose, and in fact the majority of all breeds (including crossbreeds and mongrels) will attempt to do so. We have known many dogs, regarded by their owners as "big softies", who surprised their owners when put to the test.

If you have a Rottweiler, German Shepherd Dog, Dobermann Pinscher or other guarding breed you might wish to go in for working trials, where the dog can partake in tracking and police work. Schutzhund training is very popular in the USA and Europe. Some breeds, such as those mentioned, have been bred specifically as guards and have a much stronger than average guarding instinct. Instead of waiting for something to happen, they tend to anticipate it and take action to prevent it happening. In some countries this is acceptable, but a dog of this type needs experienced handling. There are some breeds, classed as Sheepdogs and usually

The four Collie breeds: the Border, the Bearded, the Rough and the Smooth.

originating in Europe or Asia, that do not herd in the same way as the Border Collie. They have been bred to stay with the flock and guard it against all predators, whether on two legs or four. Maremma Sheepdogs and Pyrenean Mountain Dogs (Great Pyrenees) come into this category and are being used very successfully in Canada and the USA as well as in Europe.

THE TERRIER BREEDS
The enormous range of terriers have all been bred to kill vermin, such as rats and rabbits. As the name suggests, most terriers are expected to go to ground and tackle foxes and other formidable adversaries. So terriers were expected to be tough and active, and have a strong killing instinct. This does not mean that every terrier wants to kill everything he sees. For example, he will happily spend a day rabbiting alongside a ferret. If you know anyone who will let you have a day's rabbiting on their land, the chances are that your terrier will be delighted to help.

UNDERSTANDING INSTINCTS

Instincts have no relationship to intelligence. For instance, we might take two sheepdogs: one dog is not very intelligent but has a strong herding instinct; the other dog is exceptionally intelligent but with a weak herding instinct. The strong instinct in the first dog will make him keep on trying, and by constant repetition, he will learn what is wanted of him. The second dog cannot be bothered with all that repetition, and because of his intelligence, he can think of other things he would rather do. It is the dog with the strong working instinct who can always be relied on to do something, even if it is not quite what was wanted.

Instinct is something which is either present or not present. It cannot be put there, and it cannot be taken away. It may lie dormant until roused by some stimulus. A retriever pup may ignore a ball lying on the ground; kick the ball, and the pup will almost certainly run after it and pick it up. Once he has done this, he will become more interested in the ball even when it is lying still.

A dog – any dog – may ignore a flock of sheep, quietly grazing. But if they run, his hunting instinct will immediately take over. This will be strengthened by the presence of another dog, which forms a pack, and this increases the risk of attack by more than fifty per cent. Most important of all is the fact that an instinct strengthens with use. If a dog has always ignored cyclists and then suddenly decides to chase one, you can be absolutely certain that he will want to chase the next cyclist he sees. Every time he does, it reduces the chance of breaking the habit.

We have devoted so much space to the subject of instincts because it is so often misunderstood. We hear of dogs who have "turned nasty" for no reason – when the reason is perfectly obvious. There is the terrier who kills the neighbour's pet rabbit and the owner just cannot understand it: "He is such a sweet little dog and so good with the children." Worse still is the owner who leaves a dog alone with an infant, whose actions, noises, and smell are much more akin to a wild animal, as far as the dog is concerned. Every owner should make an effort to understand the instincts which are present in their dog, bearing in mind that the strength of the instincts varies. Whether it is an asset or a liability, an instinct can be controlled by training and by diverting it into other channels. If it is to be an asset, it should be encouraged as soon as it makes an appearance. If it is likely to be a liability – sadly more often the case with pet dogs – you must be ready to control it the very first time it shows.

Chapter Seven

TRAINING EXERCISES

Different people want their pups to learn different things, but it is fairly safe to say that most people want a dog who is clean in the house, walks quietly on a lead, sits and lies down on command, and comes when called.

THE RECALL
Before tackling this exercise, let us first solve the problem of why so many dogs refuse to come when called. The answer is that their owners have taught them not to respond. This is almost certainly unintentional, but the result is the same. It happens in many ways, such as calling the puppy, and then shouting when he does not come because he is investigating a fascinating new scent. When the pup eventually decides that he has satisfied his curiosity, he returns to his owner who promptly grabs hold of him, and scolds him for not coming when called.

But as far as the pup is concerned, he has been told off for coming – as that was the last thing he did. It was the legendary dog trainer Barbara Woodhouse who said: "You can't compete with a smell on a gatepost!" So, bearing this in mind, always attract your pup's attention before you call him. Always call him in a happy, cheerful voice, and praise him well when he comes to you. Do not keep on calling him for no reason; if you keep on shouting his name, he will soon treat it like any other background noise, such as the radio.

As already mentioned, dogs understand sounds, not words, and they associate certain sounds with certain actions. One of the first, if not *the* first, association which any puppy should learn is that if he responds to his name he will be rewarded. Use food as a reward, but not every time. Food is very useful, especially for puppies, but your object is to have a dog who obeys whether you have food or not. Your pup should never demand food for doing a certain action. If he is only given food at odd intervals, then he will not come to regard it as a right.

If you allow your puppy free-running exercise, it is essential that he does not stray too far from you, and is responsive to the recall. Do not wait too long before you give your puppy a taste of freedom; it is much easier to teach a puppy to stay with you before his instincts have developed. The hunting instinct will encourage the pup to chase anything that runs, and the sex instinct will make him mark his territory, sniff around trees, and develop other 'pastimes' which are certainly not for your benefit.

To help you counterbalance these instincts, there is the submissive instinct which makes the pup want to please his owner. In some cases, this is so strong that it makes the dog more anxious to obey his owner than to follow his other instincts.

Owners of such dogs wonder what all the fuss is about when their dog never shows any tendency to leave them – but they do not know how lucky they are!

We are often told of the importance of preventing bad habits, but seldom of the importance of developing good ones. If a puppy strays too far from you, but is recalled and immediately well-rewarded every time he comes to you, he should soon develop the habit of staying within range. If he chases a squirrel or a rabbit, make sure he comes right back to you, and make equally sure that you reward him for doing so. A good way of encouraging a pup to keep an eye on you is to hide behind a tree or bush when he is not looking. However, make sure that you can still see your puppy, as when he finds you are not there he might panic and take off in the wrong direction. If he does that you will have to call him, but otherwise let him find you. Most puppies will quickly do this, using their noses.

LEAD TRAINING

Although you had your pup on a collar and lead to bring him home, he should learn to walk properly as soon as possible. Many pups do not bother at all when a collar is first put on, but others scratch and generally protest for quite a while. Just ignore all the drama, the pup will accept the collar in time. Make sure you use a light, soft collar; it should not be too tight, nor so slack that the pup can get it off or get his jaw caught in it. Always take the collar off at night.

You should not start lead training until your puppy will follow you without being on a lead. The lead is not something to make a dog go with the owner; it is a safety line to prevent him running away, and a means of controlling him when he is learning new exercises. If your pup struggles when you first put the lead on him, do not fight with him or drag him after you. Stand still, and as soon as the puppy relaxes, make a great fuss of him and encourage him with food to come up to you. Walk on a little way, holding a treat in your hand, which should encourage the puppy to follow you.

Most pups are soon trotting along quite happily, some so happily that they start pulling – a habit which needs stopping straight away. If the pup pulls, give him a sharp jerk, not a hefty one to throw him head-over-heels. Once he has stopped, call him back to you, praise him well and start off again. You could also try standing still as soon as the puppy starts pulling. It takes two to pull, and the pup will not get any fun out of it if you will not 'play.' Once the puppy is behaving, tell him he is a good boy and start walking again, talking to him and trying to keep his attention. Make it fun; you are not teaching drill, you are teaching your puppy to walk along beside you quietly. It is important that the pup looks forward to going for a walk on the lead.

THE SIT

Teach the 'Sit' before the 'Down'. Call your puppy to you and when you have his attention, hold your hand just above his head, at the same time saying "Sit". As the pup looks up, move your hand towards the back of his head and as his eyes follow your hand movements, he should automatically sit. As soon as he sits, give him a treat and praise him well, but not too enthusiastically as this will make him excited and he may get up.

If the puppy shows signs of moving, place your hand on his rump to keep him there for a few seconds. Then tell him "OK" and let him get up. Repeat this four or

ABOVE:Training cannot start too early. These five-week-old puppies are already running to the sound they associate with food. This is the early beginnings of teaching the Recall.

BELOW: In a more formal situation, this Chihuahua puppy is being taught the Recall, using food as a reward.

Lead training can start in the garden before the puppy has completed his full course of inoculations. Food can be used to encourage the puppy to walk in the same direction as the owner.

It is a good idea to introduce control and discipline at an early age. This puppy is being kept on a lead until both child and pup are happy with each other.

five times, but do not keep on or he will only get fed up. When you have finished the lesson, have a game together.

THE DOWN

Once your puppy knows how to sit on command, you can start teaching him the 'Down'. First, command your puppy to sit and attract his attention. Hold your hand, with a treat in it, in front of the pup's head, say "Down" and lower your hand to the ground just in front of him. As he goes down, praise him and give him the treat. Place your other hand on the puppy's shoulders to keep him there a moment before letting him up. If he is reluctant about going down, use your other hand from the start to press down on his shoulders.

Both the 'Sit'and the 'Down' can be taught whenever you have a few spare minutes. However, make sure you do not always teach these exercises in the same place, otherwise you will end up with a puppy who thinks he should only lie down in the kitchen and sit in the lounge!

PLAY TRAINING

Once your puppy has mastered the basic exercises, you may wish to teach him some play exercises. This will be fun for you and your family, and it will result in a happier dog who receives plenty of stimulation and is eager to respond to his owner.

JUMPING

Teaching jumping too early can harm a growing puppy, and no dog should attempt hurdles and the other obstacles used on agility courses until fully mature. However, few puppies will damage themselves jumping or scrambling over fallen trees, ditches or banks on a country walk. In fact, you would probably have trouble stopping a young dog doing this. However, you must never encourage the pup to tackle anything too ambitious, not only because he might get hurt, but because it will probably put him off for life. If you have an Old English Sheepdog, covered with mud on a wet day, and you have to lift him over a fence or stile, you will certainly wish you had not put him off jumping!

When your pup is a bit older, you can put up small jumps in the garden and teach him to jump properly. Decide on a word of command, such as "Over" or "Hup". Broom handles are useful for making small, light jumps. Put the jump next to a fence so the pup cannot get round one side of it. To start with, hop over the jump yourself, encouraging the pup to come with you. If he responds, reward him well. If not, then try putting the puppy on a long lead to prevent him running past the jump – not to drag him over it. Make sure the pup is jumping freely before gradually increasing the height of the jump. Do not forget: no high jumps for young puppies. If the pup is keen on retrieving, it often helps to throw a ball or toy over for him to fetch. Try to find different obstacles on your walks; like us, dogs get fed up with the same thing and they enjoy some variety.

Even small dogs can be taught a selection of jumping tricks, such as over your leg, or a stick, through a hoop or through your arms. Older children can have great fun playing with a dog in this way. Once your puppy jumps on command, these tricks are usually easy to teach. Start off with a stick. Put your pup back on the lead, hold the stick fairly low in front of him, and tell him to jump. Once he is jumping well, take the lead off. The pup can progress from this to jumping over your leg. First, hold out your leg with the stick alongside it. Once he jumps this, remove the stick and the pup should jump over your leg.

Before you teach your puppy to jump through your arms, teach him to jump through a hoop. A piece of one-inch plastic hose, bent into a circle and secured, makes a safe, cheap hoop. Hold the hoop, low to the ground in front of your puppy and encourage him to go through it. It is best to use a different command, as the pup is not going over a jump but through it. If he is doubtful, throw a treat through. To progress to jumping through your arms, simply circle the hoop in your arms and, with any luck, your puppy will jump through. If he seems muddled, ask someone to help by holding the hoop for you, and put him back on a lead until he does it properly.

Small dogs can be taught to jump into your arms. So can big ones – but we do not recommend this for little old ladies with large Rottweilers! To start with, squat down with the puppy in front of you, give him a command, patting your knees excitedly and try to persuade him to climb up. Once he is doing this, try to get him to jump up. Next, stand up but keep your knees bent and hold your hands low, so that you can catch him as he jumps. Finally, stand upright and catch your pup – but make very sure he never falls.

SHAKING HANDS

Perhaps the simplest trick of all is shaking hands. In fact, some dogs do it without ever being taught. Puppies instinctively knead at their mother's teats to stimulate the milk-flow. Once the pups are older, the bitch often stands up in response to this kneading and prodding. The pups then usually sit underneath her and suckle while reaching up with their paws. So giving a paw is simply an extension of this natural action.

If your pup is the sort who offers up a paw, take it and reward him with a treat, giving him a command at the same time. Soon he should realise that this action pleases you, and he should do it every time you ask him. If your puppy is not a 'natural', you may have to start by giving a command and tapping his leg until he lifts it. When he responds, make a great fuss of him and reward him. Be warned: there is a snag with teaching a dog to shake hands. Some become obsessed with it and try to do it all the time, becoming perfect pests. So make sure your puppy only does it when asked, and stops when told to.

BEGGING

This is something else which should not be taught too soon. It puts a strain on the back of an immature pup, especially a long-legged breed. However, as with shaking hands, some pups teach themselves to beg. Small, stocky pups are less likely to damage themselves but you must still be careful. With a small dog, all that is usually needed is to have him sit, tell him to beg, hold a treat just above his head and encourage him to sit up. If this does not work, treat him as you would a larger breed.

Take your puppy to a corner, which will support his back as he sits up. Tell him to sit, hold his front paws in one hand and tell him to beg, holding a treat over his head with the other hand. Then gently lift his front paws up until he is in the right position. Make sure he is properly balanced. Once the puppy starts to go up on his

Teach the Sit before the Down. Hold your hand above the puppy's head, give the command "Sit", and as he looks up, move your hand towards the back of his head. As he follows your hand signals, the puppy should automatically sit.

This is a natural progression from the Sit. When your puppy is sitting, attract his attention with a tidbit, and then lower your hand downwards, giving the command "Down".

These five-week-old pups are suckling from their mother. Note how they naturally use their paws. This is an instinct which can be useful when teaching a pup to shake hands, or later on, to trigger a flyball pedal.

If you want to teach your puppy to retrieve, the instinct must be encouraged. Do not make the mistake of telling your puppy off if he 'retrieves' a forbidden object. Praise him for bringing it to you, and then substitute it with a toy that is allowed.

own, be ready to support him if he loses his balance. Like many tricks, some dogs learn this quickly but others will need a lot of your patience.

CATCHING
We have always taught our dogs to catch food thrown to them, which makes it easy to get them to stand 'to attention' in front of a judge. It also makes it easy to reward a dog immediately he does what is wanted. A lot of dogs are natural catchers, others fail to see the point at all. It is best to start with food. Call the pup to you, stand a little way back, tell him to catch, making sure he is watching your hand, and throw or half-drop the treat towards his mouth.

If your puppy misses, pick up the treat, do not let him have it, and try again. If he manages to catch it, stop, and start again next day. As your puppy improves, gradually stand further back until he will catch it from quite a distance. Once he is catching well, he can be taught to catch a ball – make sure it is large enough so that he cannot swallow it – and later on, you can play frisbee with him. If your puppy shows an aptitude for catching you may like to try him at flyball when he is fully grown.

SPEAK ON COMMAND
This is not really a trick as it has many practical uses, such as warning you when visitors arrive. Watch your pup and try to find out what makes him bark. It may be when he is going for a walk, when you start playing with him, when the doorbell rings, or when he wants his dinner. When your puppy does bark, tell him "Speak" and reward him. Put a lot of enthusiasm into it, as you want him to be excited. Even if it takes a while, this is well worth teaching. In fact, the easiest way to stop a noisy dog from barking is to teach him to bark on command – and then to teach him to stop barking!

HIDE-AND-SEEK
Puppies are very like children, and hide-and-seek is a very successful shared game. All dogs have far better 'noses' than humans and most enjoy using them. We have a Chihuahua whose perseverance at finding hidden objects would surprise many people with working trials dogs.

Start off by playing hide-and-seek with children doing the hiding, and you can then progress to hiding a toy or some other object. This will be easier with the retriever breeds, who love holding something in their mouths. Start by throwing the object out a short distance where the puppy can see it, and send him to fetch it. Increase the distance, and throw the object into long grass where the pup has to look for it.

You can also try dropping a glove or something similar behind you when out for a walk. Do this when the pup is ahead of you, call him back and encourage him to go and find it. Soon, he should be able to go back quite a distance. Although this exercise is basically a game, it can develop into a very useful exercise. More than once we have been very grateful when one of our dogs has found our lost car keys or gloves.

RETRIEVING
Of all the useful exercises you can teach your puppy, retrieving must be of more benefit than any other to the average pet dog owner. Like the hunting instinct, the

retrieving instinct is present in virtually all dogs of all breeds. The wild dog kills its prey, very often in the open, picks it up and hurriedly carries it to the nearest cover where he is less likely to be seen by rival predators, or food might be carried back to the den for the pups. By careful selective breeding, man has strengthened the retrieving instinct so that in some breeds of gundogs we find puppies which cannot help picking up anything they can carry.

As mentioned earlier, instincts strengthen with use and weaken, or even die, if not used. The age at which instincts make their first appearance varies between breeds and individuals; if the instinct is to develop it should be encouraged at the earliest stage. Failure to do so is the main reason why some dogs appear to have no retrieving instinct. A puppy picks up something and rushes around, but if he is continually ignored then he will probably stop bothering to retrieve at all.

Then, worse still, the puppy brings something to you and is scolded for being "naughty." This may well be a natural reaction if the pup brings you a very dead, very smelly rabbit when you are out for a walk, or if he greets you with one of your best shoes in his mouth. But, just as puppies have to learn to control their natural reactions, so must we. While the retrieving instinct is developing – the 'seedling stage' so to speak – the puppy must be praised every time he shows any inclination to pick something up. Once he retrieves on command, he should only be rewarded when he retrieves in response to your order to do so. Some dogs becomes obsessive about retrieving, and not everyone wants to go for a walk with a dog that never stops dropping stones, sticks, etc., at their feet.

There are several methods of teaching the retrieve, but we will concentrate on the play method. This is really just a question of encouraging the retrieving instinct, rather than teaching a specific action, as we do when teaching the 'Down'. Here the operative word is 'play'. Children can often encourage a puppy to retrieve far quicker than their parents. They are less inhibited and do not feel they are "making fools of themselves" by talking baby language, or even getting on all fours to encourage the puppy to play. Many adults have great difficulty behaving like a puppy, especially in the company of others. However, the children must be supervised. A puppy will not learn to retrieve if the children throw a ball, and then chase him all around the garden trying to grab it back.

The object you use to teach the retrieve does not really matter, so long as you choose something that the puppy likes and which is easy to carry. Never try to force him to pick up something which he obviously dislikes. Use something which is easy for both of you to hold, such as a stuffed sock or a soft toy. Odd though it sounds, it is much easier to teach a puppy to let go of something he likes, than to teach him to hold on to something which he has decided he would rather spit out! If the puppy refuses to release the object, a treat offered on a fair exchange basis will usually persuade him to let go.

The aim of every dog owner must be to train their dog to be a well-behaved member of society, who will fit in with a variety of different situations.

Chapter Eight

GROWING UP

THE NEED FOR DISCIPLINE
In the human race, adolescence is widely recognised as a problematic time for youngsters, a time when the body undergoes major physical changes, and as maturity approaches, parental authority is challenged. Some teenagers are more prone to get into serious trouble at this stage, and this is often attributed to lack of discipline in childhood, and lack of useful employment and stimulation. Very much the same applies to dogs.

It is normal for puppies to be disciplined by their mother for as long as they are with her. If this discipline is continued by the new owner, the pups are less likely to cause trouble when they become 'teenagers', than those who have been allowed to

A puppy needs to learn his place in the family.

run wild. In the early stages, most of the training can be applied by reward, whereas later on some correction will almost certainly be necessary.

REACHING ADOLESCENCE
The age at which a puppy becomes adolescent varies between breeds and individuals of the same breed. Generally speaking, small breeds mature much more quickly than large ones. Yorkshire Terriers are quite often as mature at six months as some Irish Wolfhounds are at two years. The level of testosterone, especially in the male, is at its peak at about this time. Quite suddenly, this can make the pup feel 'grown up', and that there is much more to life than obeying his owner. The opposite sex becomes more interesting and the marking of territory more important. Signs of dominance may appear for the first time, and sometimes the first signs of aggression, especially towards other dogs.

This subject is rarely discussed, with the result that owners are taken by surprise and think that something has "gone wrong", when it is a perfectly natural process of growing up. If you realise this, and treat your dog as a young adult rather than a puppy, you should not have a great problem.

THE IN-SEASON BITCH
The first indication of adolescence in the bitch is when she first comes in season. The age at which this happens varies considerably, some coming in season as early as six months and others not until twelve months or older. This is a very traumatic experience for the bitch. Not only does she have to cope with hormonal changes, which affect her both mentally and physically, it is also inevitable that her lifestyle will change to some degree.

For a start, she will have to be kept away from male dogs. Quite apart from the sexual attraction of the moment, some of these dogs may have been her friends and playmates since puppyhood. Suddenly, and for no reason that she can understand, she is not allowed to see them at all. Not surprisingly, the behaviour of some bitches changes dramatically at this stage, and occasionally the change is permanent.

It is important to do everything possible to prevent the bitch from feeling that she is no longer wanted. No attempt should be made to teach new exercises, especially any lessons that she does not like very much. Make more effort to play games with her, and indulge in anything she enjoys doing.

THE CASE FOR NEUTERING
Neutering remains a highly controversial subject, with potential for an endless source of debate. Today the English Kennel Club allows neutered animals of both sexes to be entered at shows. This move has been severely criticised by many breeders, but it is hard to understand why this should be the case. At most horse shows geldings far outnumber stallions, and at cat shows there are classes for neuters.

Unless we want to use an individual for breeding, all our dogs are castrated and our bitches are spayed. We have found that any change in behaviour – and there is very little change – is for the better as far as the owner is concerned. All Guide Dogs for the Blind, of both sexes, are neutered with no adverse effects.

There is some difference of opinion as to the best age to operate. Many vets recommend castration before the puppy is four months old, arguing that it is a simpler operation at that age. But vets do not live with their patients and rarely know what changes have taken place. Our own observations suggest that dogs castrated too soon fail to mature mentally. They lack initiative and they are liable to obesity, which does not happen if castration is left until the dog matures. The best guide to this is when the dog starts lifting his leg. Our own bitches are not spayed until after their first season. However, we have known of bitches spayed at around six or seven months when they had not come in season, with no ill effects.

Apart from the advantages to the owner, neutering can be a benefit to the animal itself. Few pet dogs ever have the opportunity to mate a bitch, but many have to suffer the frustration caused by the presence of a bitch in season living within close proximity. Bitches endure the trauma of solitary confinement every six months – for life. Spaying removes the necessity for this, and it also removes the risk of pyometra, an illness common among older breeding bitches.

DOMINANCE

In a dog pack there are varying degrees of dominance, but there is always one dominant leader. Fortunately for us, the dog is quite happy to allow the human animal to take on the role of leader, and there is no shortage of advice as to how this should be done. Nevertheless, some important points are often overlooked.

Some dogs are born to be leaders, but, as with humans, the majority are quite happy to be led. The idea that every puppy must be dominated from the word go leads to many submissive puppies failing to develop initiative. Far from being dominated, such puppies must be brought out of themselves if they are to develop into confident adults.

Dominance is relative. A dog that is dominant towards one person may be submissive towards another. Many dogs are dominant towards one member of the family and submissive towards another. The person who finds it difficult to control their own small children will inevitably fail with a dominant dog. However, they may form a perfectly good relationship with a more submissive type who has no desire to challenge their authority.

We believe that dominance has come to the fore partly as a result of the modern cult of the 'kind' trainer. We are certainly not advocating unkind or even harsh training: respect, not fear, should be the aim. In any case, cruelty or kindness are terms which cannot readily be defined – they mean different things to different people. For instance, the electric training collar is regarded by many people with deep suspicion and they believe it has no place in any humane training programme. However, we came into contact with an Afghan bitch who worried sheep, and she was to be destroyed. After one lesson with an electric collar, the bitch would not go near a sheep. She lived a long and happy life – we leave it to you to decide whether this treatment was cruel.

What is cruel to one dog is not at all cruel to another. For instance, to jerk a Whippet or a Greyhound on a chain slip collar would be extremely cruel, but a Bull Terrier would not even feel it. Different breeds have different responses, and within each breed there is a whole range of temperaments. The successful dog owner assesses a dog on the basis of observation, rather than trying to apply dog training theories, regardless of the dog's individual character.

A dominant dog does not necessarily represent a failure on the part of the owner; over the years we have had many dominant dogs, including some of our very best workers. If the pup with a dominant nature is correctly reared and trained (as

All puppies should have an elementary education while they are still young, particularly if you have a giant breed such as a St Bernard.

Never forget the importance of stimulation. An active, intelligent dog, such as the German Shepherd Dog, will enjoy being presented with new training challenges.

If you achieve a balanced relationship with your dog, when he happily accepts you as pack leader, you can look forward to years of pleasurable companionship together.

outlined in earlier chapters), a relationship of mutual respect is established and there is no reason why any problems should arise.

A BALANCED RELATIONSHIP

The aim of every dog owner is to achieve a happy, balanced relationship with their dog. The dog should respect the 'pack leader', and be secure in the knowledge that he is a valued member of the pack – but not *the* most important member.

Many canine behaviourists believe that this ideal situation will be more easily achieved if a number of rules are observed. For example, the owner should assert authority by always eating before the pup is fed. The theory behind this is that the pack leader always eats first. But in the wild, the bitch and some of the subordinate members of the pack will carry food in their stomachs and regurgitate it for the puppies. The bitch will still do this when she herself is short of food. It is the puppies who are given 'special' treatment. All the puppies we rear have their breakfast first thing in the morning, before we eat and before the adult dogs are fed. In fact, the adults look on while the pup is feeding.

Another modern theory is that you must never allow a dog to sleep on your bed or to go on chairs. However, many people allow this behaviour, and we have found no evidence that this encourages a dog to be dominant. It is a matter of personal preference, depending on what the owner finds acceptable – and the state of the furniture! Our dogs are allowed to sit on some chairs but not on others. They very quickly learn which are "their" chairs. The important point is that whether it be sleeping on the bed, sitting on a chair, going through a door, getting in or out of the car, or playing with a toy, the dog does it by *your* permission.

Some people maintain that if a dog is lying on the floor, the owner should make the dog get up and move out of the way, asserting their dominance over the dog. We teach our dogs to lie still and allow us to step over them. Can anything be more submissive than lying on the floor while a human being, at least six times your height, steps over you?

COPING WITH BAD BEHAVIOUR

Just like teenagers, your adolescent dog will have good days and bad days. You will just have to learn to live with this for a while, and make the most of the good days. Sometimes your dog will behave like an overgrown puppy, and another day he will think he is a "big macho dog" who has no intention of obeying you at all.

In this situation, do not fight with him – it will only make matters worse. Above all, never give a command that you are that is likely to be ignored, and that you cannot enforce. The best remedy is to play with your dog – games such as chasing a ball or playing hide-and-seek with a favourite toy – and generally providing plenty of exercise.

Although your dog may not realise it, he is still getting some training, although he is enjoying himself and sees it all as fun. However, if the dog persists in doing things that you really cannot allow, put him on a lead, command him to go in the Down, and make sure he stays in that position for a reasonably long period. No exercise has a sobering effect on a dog.

Remember that young dogs have a very short attention span. So do not start giving long training sessions; your dog will only become bored and will be easily distracted. Keep training sessions short and cheerful, always ending on a good, positive note. You will achieve far more in this situation than if you keep nagging at your dog in long, tedious training sessions. You also run a very real risk of your dog learning to dread training sessions – and then all progress will be at a complete standstill.

AVOIDING TEMPTATION

The adolescent dog finds it almost impossible to resist temptation, so the best course of action is to try to avoid situations where your dog is likely to disobey house rules. Do not give him the opportunity to steal the Sunday roast by leaving him alone in the kitchen. If you are going out without your dog, make sure you do not leave him in a room where he can tear up your best rug. When your cat is sitting sunning herself in the garden, do not let your dog out so he can chase it. The last thing you want at this stage is a showdown. Confrontation will start a battle of wills, and all the good work you have done building a relationship with your dog will be ruined. The vast majority of young dogs will soon settle down, and peace and harmony will be restored.

DOGS IN THE COUNTRYSIDE

There are not so many places where dogs can run free these days, but they can be found. Once your pup is old enough to go for long walks, he will enjoy being taken for free-running exercise. But he must be under complete control. A dog running free in the country must come back when called and drop instantly on command. A dog chasing a rabbit can easily end up chasing sheep.

Bear in mind how much your pup loves chasing a ball. A flock of woolly lambs skipping across a field will arouse his hunting instinct and prove far more exciting. So unless your dog has been brought up with sheep, keep him under close control if there is any livestock about. If you stop for a picnic, always tie the dog up. Never leave him running around on his own.

Be careful if you cross a field with cows in it. They are notoriously inquisitive, and may well come charging across to look at you and your dog. Just keep calm; don't shout at the cows, or the dog. Walk quietly to the gate with the dog beside you. The countryside is a pleasant place for a dog, but it is up to you to teach him to respect it and the animals that live in it.

PRAISE AND STIMULATION

If you have spent time socialising and training your puppy through his early days, you will be repaid a hundredfold. It is important to bear in mind that we all work better when we are praised, so never forget to reward and praise your dog for doing the right thing, even after he has been trained and has performed the exercise correctly on innumerable occasions. After all, why should your dog try to please you if he gets nothing in return?

Like humans, a dog never stops learning. The more you teach your dog, the more he will learn and the happier he will be. Try to make sure he has something to do – fetching your slippers, fetching the mail, barking to alert you when the door bell rings. When you go out for a walk, vary the route you take and give your dog something different to do, such as searching for a ball, swimming, jumping or retrieving. All these things will help to form a bond of friendship between you.

If you have spent time training and socialising your dog, you will be richly repaid.

Take your dog along to training classes; even if you do not end up with an Obedience champion, you can have a lot of fun, and your dog will benefit from the time you are working together. As your dog reaches maturity, you can think about some of the other activities, such as agility, working trails, or flyball. We were all brought up with the saying "the devil finds work for idle hands." Substitute paws for hands and this is equally true of your dog. A bored dog is certain to get into trouble, whereas a well-trained, well-balanced dog will be a pleasure to you and your family for the duration of his life.